CREATING
TRUST
IN AN UNDERSTANDABLY
UN-TRUSTING WORLD

CREATING TRUST

IN AN UNDERSTANDABLY UN-TRUSTING WORLD

THE SECRET DESIRES OF TODAY'S CLIENTS

AND HOW THE FINANCIAL ADVISOR
CAN PROSPER BY FULFILLING THEM

(OR BE PUNISHED OR PERISH BY IGNORING THEM)

MATT ZAGULA
WITH DAN S. KENNEDY

Advantage®

Published by Advantage, Charleston, South Carolina.
Member of Advantage Media Group.

ADVANTAGE is a registered trademark and the Advantage colophon is a trademark of Advantage Media Group, Inc.

Printed in the United States of America.

ISBN: 978-1-59932-259-9
LCCN: 2010919531

This publication is designed to provide accurate and authoritative information in regard to the subject matter covered. It is sold with the understanding that the publisher is not engaged in rendering legal, accounting, or other professional services. If legal advice or other expert assistance is required, the services of a competent professional person should be sought.

Advantage Media Group is proud to be a part of the Tree Neutral™ program. Tree Neutral offsets the number of trees consumed in the production and printing of this book by taking proactive steps such as planting trees in direct proportion to the number of trees used to print books. To learn more about Tree Neutral, please visit **www.treeneutral.com**. To learn more about Advantage's commitment to being a responsible steward of the environment, please visit **www.advantagefamily.com/green**

Advantage Media Group is a leading publisher of business, motivation, and self-help authors. Do you have a manuscript or book idea that you would like to have considered for publication? Please visit **www.amgbook.com** or call **1.866.775.1696**

WHAT IF
EVERYTHING YOU THOUGHT AND BELIEVED ABOUT SUCCESSFULLY RELATING TO CLIENTS WAS

WRONG*?

*(FOR THESE TIMES)

"Trust No One" is the new mantra. Seniors, affluent individuals, business leaders and investors have seen virtually every institution and corporate leader and even the <u>premise</u> of "homeland security" and government response to emergency prove themselves spectacularly untrustworthy, and are given sensationalized reasons daily by every media to distrust banks, insurers and others on Wall Street, so it is perfectly understandable that **they are NOT prepared to trust you,** NOT one word you say, NOT any promise you make, NOT any organization or product you represent. **Any professional advisor or agent seeking to establish new relationships and secure new clients in this environment finds himself severely handicapped,** with his chief obstacle – fully understood or not – exceptionally high, exceptionally firm and stubborn distrust. This is reflected in shrinking seminar attendance and rising costs of buying such attendance, declining response to advertising, longer sales cycles, even heightened reluctance by clients to refer, as well as lower initial transactions.

THERE <u>ARE</u> EFFECTIVE RESPONSES and strategies, but they are not the same ones that worked nicely, pre-2008. And even before tackling the subject of more appropriate and effective strategies for this time, **a new understanding of where the prospective client is,** psychologically and emotionally when you first 'arrive' is essential –and that is where this timely, groundbreaking and frank book, TRUST, begins.

ABOUT THE AUTHORS

MATT ZAGULA leads a high-income financial advisory practice in Weirton, West Virginia. The practice generates minimally $2.5-Million of revenue annually. He is the author of the book *INVASION OF THE MONEY SNATCHERS*, host of his own radio program, airing his own television infomercials, and frequently conducts public seminars in his area (although never with inducement of "free dinner"). Interestingly, he not only dominates his local market via his own direct-marketing, but is provided with client referrals by top estate and elder law attorneys in and far from his area.

In addition, he publishes *THE MILLIONAIRE ADVISOR*, consults privately with exceptionally successful advisors, and conducts coaching programs exclusively for advisors associated with Advisors Excel. He began his career in financial services in 1993, and quickly determined that much of the traditional, commonly used advertising, marketing and sales practices failed to create trust – and then began looking outside the industry for inspiration. His extensive search for the answers to "There Must Be A Better Way" led him to leading marketing experts like his co-author here, Dan Kennedy, and enabled him to create a very different, successful, profitable, stress-free practice.

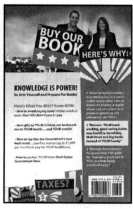

ABOUT THE AUTHORS

DAN S. KENNEDY is a celebrated author – his books appear on the *INC. MAGAZINE List of 100 Best Business Books, BUSINESS WEEK* Magazine's Bestseller List, Amazon bestseller lists, and receiving praise from *SUCCESS, ENTREPRENEUR* and *FORBES* Magazine. His books include one focused on "marketing to the affluent." Dan is a multi-millionaire, serial entrepreneur who has started, built, bought and sold businesses of his own, but he principally operates a private practice as a business/marketing strategist/consultant, coach and direct-response copywriter, every year earning a 7-figure income from fees and royalties paid by diverse clients – with 85% returning to Dan again and again. He has extensive experience guiding those in private practice and advice businesses, including doctors, lawyers, and financial advisors; extensive experience with clients marketing to seniors; and extensive experience with clients marketing investments here and abroad. He has also had a long tenure as one of the most sought after professional speakers in his subject matter, including 9 consecutive years on the #1 seminar tour in America, with audiences from 10,000 to 35,000 in each of 25+ cities a year. He also owns 20 or so harness racing horses and drives professionally in about 200 races himself. He lives in Ohio and Virginia with his 2nd and 3rd wives (one in the same) and The Million Dollar Dog. His single beleaguered assistant is in Arizona, in an office he never visits.

The Million Dollar Dog

7

COIN OF THE REALM

Owner: Kennedy Sports Corp.
Driver: Dan Kennedy   Trainer: Clair Umholtz
Condition Pace - Purse $1.600   May 29, 2010
28   57.3   1:27.3   1:58.2

NORTHFIELD PARK
LIVE AND SIMULCAST RACING
JJ ZAMAIKO PHOTOGRAPHY © 2010

Dan Kennedy Win Photo, Northfield Park, May 29, 2010

Note: Mr. Kennedy is NOT associated with Advisors Excel LLC nor with Matt Zagula or his companies. He is an exclusive guest-expert contributor to certain publications, trainings and coaching programs provided to the financial services industry by Matt Zagula.

CREATING TRUST is presented and sponsored by Advisors Excel LLC.

Advisors Excel, is the fast growth, innovative leader in insurance marketing based on one core value: Our Advisors Are Our Clients! With unmatched profit sharing and marketing reimbursement their legendary advisors are on pace to submit over $2-BILLION in direct annuity premiums this year.

Advisors Excel truly is the Major Leagues of Field Marketing Organizations. Often the number one advisor at other marketing organizations would struggle to make the top 25 on Advisors Excel's impressive leader board. If you're ready to join the Major Leagues and become part of Advisors Excel's legendary team of advisors, you can reach us at 1-866-363-9595.

Contents

Resources

DISTRUST BORN OF UN-PROSPEROUS TIMES

"The average American family has lost 9% of their household worth in just the last 3 months of 2008 – the fastest disintegration of wealth in more than 7 decades. In fact, the majority of families were reporting a drop of 25% in their household worth in the past year alone. Pretty pessimistic stuff…Our national confidence is in pieces, our personal expectations shattered. TRUST HAS COLLAPSED. We have little tolerance now for promises and pledges. We don't trust anyone anymore."

From: *WHAT AMERICANS REALLY WANT: Truth About Our Hopes, Dreams and Fears* by Dr. Frank Luntz, leading pollster and trend analyst, frequently seen on FOX.

CHAPTER 1

ASKING THE WRONG QUESTIONS

BY DAN KENNEDY

WHERE CAN I FIND CLIENTS? It is very much the wrong question. The right question is: how can you construct a business life so that clients keep finding you? I think of it as money coming out of the woodwork. A good example occurred this week. A new, prospective client called my office "out of the blue" (yet not by accident); my assistant gave him "the rules of engagement"; he subsequently faxed in his required memo, describing his situation; a preliminary phone appointment then booked. There is somewhere between $40,000.00 and $60,000.00 in this as initial fee, plus upside through royalties on several different income streams realistically worth mid-6-figures. Maybe more. I did NO prospecting to get this. So, where did this come from?

The new client was introduced to my work – books, newsletter, etc. – a handful of years ago, by a client of his who had been a member of one of my mastermind groups for three years. Two years ago, this individual attended a workshop I conducted on "marketing to the affluent" as that client's guest. He has been getting my newsletter this entire time. He matured over time as a client.

So, three important facts: first, the gestation period leading up to him calling my office was either 2 or 5 years depending on how you care to count. I would say 5. There was a referral involved. There was 2 days of experience with me in a workshop setting. There was a constant drip of continuing exposure. It took time to cook this. And I had to be "hanging around" when this opportunity finally arose in his business, that he chose to bring to me. Second, there was more than one thing involved. Ultimately, he came forward, ready to employ me *if he was able to do so.* He therefore cheerfully accepted our way of doing business. And without question, ponied up the $18,800.00 fee for an initial day. It is by being Out There a lot, in different ways, and in different media, that I draw these kinds of opportunities to me. I did nothing overt or direct to get this. Nor could I have. If hunting, I'd never have found it. If you do not have business finding you, it is because (a) you are not Out There in multiple ways in front of people who could hire you, and (b) because you are spending too much time hunting and are seen (and therefore de-valued) as a hungry hunter. **Hunting is antithetical to creating trust.** This individual trusts me and seeks me as a trusted advisor, because he has come to trust me at his pace, over time, through multiple exposures and experiences.

Of course I understand that many instantly reject this or judge it bad news. "You don't understand," whines the hungry hunter, "I need something to eat today, not 3 years from now, and my pantry is empty. This is fine for you, Kennedy, but no good for me." If you permit that thinking, if you allow yourself to be totally consumed by your urgent and pressing hunger, then 3 years from now, you'll still be opening the door to an empty pantry, still be trying to hunt down today's meal today, still consumed by your urgent needs, and still giving off the stench of desperation. Here's how to change your thinking: take a piece of paper and divide it in thirds, in vertical columns. They get these three headers: Short-Term/Now, Medium-Term/2 to 3 Years, and Long-Term/3 to 5 Years. Make investments of thought, time, energy, effort, work, output and money in all three places, simultaneously, every day, now. You can weight it to Short-Term if really, really hungry. I get it: I have eaten only the dinner the spare change unearthed from couch and car seat would buy, so I'm speaking about this literally not just figuratively. That little weight-loss program was necessary at the time in part because I was investing money I did not have into mailings into a target market creating familiarity and prominence on which I knew I could not begin collecting until Medium-Term. (Stallone turned down three different offers of $50,000.00 for his original Rocky script, even though he and his pregnant wife were living in a one room apartment and had no money – because he was determined to also star in the movie, and would not let loose of the script without that wholly unreasonable demand, the casting of an unknown, first-time actor as star, included in the deal. It takes a certain doggedness to go hungry like that by choice. You find it as a behavioral characteristic and back-story in just about every exceptionally successful individual.)

Yes, you <u>can</u> hunt successfully. Hunt vigorously and get clients quickly, from just a week or month long hunt. I have. You can. And you can take comfort that most are too lazy to be in your way. If you must hunt, by all means, hunt and hunt aggressively and expansively. But AT THE VERY SAME TIME, work at not needing to hunt as much, and AT THE VERY SAME TIME, work at never needing to hunt again.

The objective is to efficiently create trust, from distrustful prospects and clients, in untrusting times. The better you get at this, the less hunting you'll need to do.

Trust is the pre-requisite for obtaining clients, opening accounts, and for subsequent client compliance and retention, and for referrals. It is the stock and trade of the legitimate advisor and con artists alike, and to pitchmen of things other than investments and financial services, to broadcasters, even to magicians.

We will get to the practical methodology of trust, I promise, but first I'd like to give you some examples of the power of trust.

A company called Salton had a patented product that, for years, languished on store shelves, creating barely enough sales volume for its survival, and that pretty much concentrated to just a few months a year, during the holiday shopping season. It was a stovetop grill. Only after pairing it with George Foreman did it skyrocket to the #1 all-time bestselling and most popular kitchen gadget. After several years of receiving royalties as high as $5-million a month, George sold his royalty interest back to the manufacturer for $125-million. No athlete – not even Michael Jordan or Tiger Woods – has ever signed a single endorsement contract worth over $100-million. Foreman holds the record for oldest boxer to win the heavyweight boxing champion title, and the record for the largest commercial endorsement fee ever paid an athlete. Yet, here's a little-known, fascinating fact: the first infomercial made for this product starring George did not do well. It opened with a couple minutes of film of George boxing, establishing him as a celebrity. Women said it turned them off and they didn't see what it had to do with the grill. Salton replaced that opening with a new one featuring George with his large family. Sales soared. The rest is rich history. Why did this near-dead, uninteresting product become a billion dollar asset? Simply because people trust George Foreman.

They believed him when he enthusiastically extolled the virtues of the odd little grilling machine. They believed he meant it, about his "personal" guarantee, evidenced by his signature on the machine itself. They believed him when he showed them his entire family in the kitchen, enjoying burgers he prepared on the grill. Because he was a champion athlete still in reasonably good shape, they believed him when he explained the health benefits of draining away the grease and fat.

Some celebrities are trusted by the public. Others are not. Having worked with advertising, direct-mail and infomercial campaigns involving nearly 100 different Hollywood and sports celebrities, I understand how special and valuable this trust is. The right star must be matched with the right product and the right demographic audience. My one-time client, Joan Rivers, out-sells just about anybody on the home shopping channel, QVC, because the women who shop there know her, believe in her as a teller of truth (even in her comedy), want to call in and talk with her, and trust her when she tells them about a product. Many other celebrities fail miserably on QVC – even those far more famous. While the public may be fascinated with them, the public doesn't trust them. Or doesn't accept the kind of product the celebrity is associated with. In short, the public "smells a rat." This is an interesting illustration of the **fragility of trust.** Everybody knows every celebrity endorsing or selling a product is being paid to do so, but that known fact does not discredit that celebrity or his or her endorsement as long as the viewer/reader/customer can also believe that celebrity genuinely likes, believes in, and preferably, uses the product. This is one of the TRUST FACTORS that people are looking for, that we'll discuss in this book: *authenticity.*

For many years, CBS dominated the TV ratings – and thus got the best advertisers and most ad dollars – for the evening news, presented by Walter Cronkite, dubbed "the most trusted man in America." The trust he had developed with the American people was an enormously valuable asset for CBS, and for its advertisers. CBS has gone downhill in this department since Cronkite's exit, with Rather, now with Katie Couric. Of course, the TV landscape has changed radically, and the nightly news is fundamentally an antiquated product given the proliferate dissemination of news all day long via a plethora of media, and the diffusion of audience from three competing networks to the cable universe. But this does not change the fact that CBS went from having the highest trust, to having negligible trust, and being nearly irrelevant. Of the same time period and lasting longer, Paul Harvey had extremely high trust with a large and diverse audience, was the most effective commercial spokesperson on radio, and was able to be a market-maker for a number of advertisers. Replicating the kind of across-the-board, universal trust that Cronkite or Harvey engendered is, I think, a practical impossibility in today's media environment. Instead, what is very instructive, is you see individuals who profit enormously by **cultivating high trust with a relatively small, narrower, like-minded audience.** Limbaugh and Beck, as examples; multi-millionaires by zealously "preaching to the converted." This is important, because it ties to another of the TRUST FACTORS you need to use: SHARED BACKGROUND OR BELIEFS.

Paul Harvey held high trust with a large but still homogenous audience, the core of which were World War II era men and women with heartland of America, patriotic and work ethic values who responded to plain talk and common sense, and leaned to the right politically. Because he was of them and in sync with them, and mirrored* their values, thoughts and conversation amongst themselves, he was trusted by them. And, for Paul, that trust was the basis of his career, business and fortune.

(*MIRRORING is a sales technique dating back the 1920's, but more recently popularized as part of NLP, Neuro-Linguistic Programming.)

Of course you'll be quick to remind me that you are not a radio or TV personality or a pitchman for cooking gadgets. What you need to understand is that these people I've just talked about are not of the news, entertainment, broadcasting, home shopping TV, or kitchen gadget businesses, but in the trust business. As are you. In your case, certain financial products are your deliverables. In my case, direct marketing consulting and copywriting are my primary deliverables (equating to 7-figure yearly income). In George Foreman's case, the countertop grille was the deliverable. But we are all selling trust. We are all in the trust business. Once you come to grips with that, then the elements of trust built and owned by any person, product or organization are useful and significant to you, and you are liberated to learn and borrow the very best strategies and techniques.

We can put a permanent end to "Where can I find clients?"

THEY ARE MORE AFRAID THAN THEY APPEAR

"People are reluctant to choose and act out of fear. Fears vary. Fear of financial losses, fear of embarrassment, fear of a self-esteem wound by feeling stupid…consequently, TRUST is THE single most important factor in marketing to the affluent."

From: Dan Kennedy's *NO BS MARKETING TO THE AFFLUENT* book.

CHAPTER 2

DON'T TEACH
UNLESS YOU WANT A TEACHER'S WAGES

BY DAN KENNEDY

Too many facts work against you. Too much explanation creates anxiety, confusion, and a sense of need to delay, to mull things over, to sort things out.

You are <u>not</u> an educator, so your goal should <u>not</u> be comprehension and understanding. You are a salesperson, with a goal of trust, then a sale, then a trusting and dependent client. The two roles are in conflict, not complementary. This is a difficult thing to accept for many, but it is reality nonetheless. The idea of "educating clients" has been advocated, maybe even popularized in your industry, but it is worship of a false god; pursuit of both an unachievable and unproductive objective. To borrow a quote usually used in another context, "it is unwise to try and teach pigs to sing; it merely annoys the pig and gets you covered with slop." I do not mean to literally compare clients to pigs, but to point out they have their own concerns – just as pigs do – that do not center around being knowledgeable, informed and smart about investing.

21

Your goal is be a good guy and keep them and their money safe from bad guys. But not to try and interest them in something inherently uninteresting to them, and an annoying distraction from their lives – work, career, business, family, friends and hobbies. You will not gain trust by fighting to turn their attention away from their interests so that you can educate them. You cannot make yourself attractive in that way.

Of course I understand, by law, your clients must have a certain level of understanding of the actual financial products they buy and investments they make, and you must meet that legally required *minimum* standard. But that, really, has to do with disclosure, not understanding.

This also does *not* preclude "informational selling," in seminars, speeches, books, articles, etc., but that is selling, not teaching, with goals divorced from transferring knowledge and expertise. The goal is trust of you (and dependence on you). Matt and I are both practitioners and advocates of "informational selling" as a positioning tool, as "bait" to attract certain prospects, and as reassurance – but never as education.

Let me take you with me to a day in Hawaii that shocked an astute Microsoft executive senseless, then we'll return to your business. I am at Joe Sugarman's on-beach mansion in Maui. You might know of Joe in connection with Blu-Blockers® sunglasses, the source of his latest fortune. Joe actually pre-dates The Sharper Image as a direct marketer of new gadgets – in fact, he was the first to advertise and sell electronic calculators. Anyway, I'm at Joe's, to speak at, and attend a small gathering of direct marketing professionals, each having paid $15,000.00 for the 3 days. By chance, on his early morning walk, Joe meets a top V.P. of Microsoft, and quickly convinces the guy to take an hour out of his vacation and come talk to us about the internet, internet marketing, the new media and the brave, new world Microsoft foresaw. When we returned from lunch to the conference room in Joe's home-complex, I saw – to my horror – that the hapless Microsoft exec had prepared huge, complex diagrams on more than two dozen sheets of poster paper and plastered the walls with them. He began droning on about nitty-gritty details – but was quickly, rudely interrupted by a leader in home-shopping TV, who worked with QVC, who stood and hollered: "Hey buddy, I sell a billion dollars a year of stuff on QVC but I couldn't care less how the picture moves from the studio to the satellite tower to the moon and back to Aunt Millie's living room. Kennedy here sells more than a billion dollars of stuff with direct-mail but has never visited a paper mill. Let's just skip to the part of how we all make money online." This sparked mutiny among the marketers, and the dazed and frightened Microsoft suit had to be quickly escorted to safety.

It is very important to understand your audience (prospect, client) – *and what THEY want to know.*

As I watched this unfold, I thought of two things – one, Napoleon Hill's* story of Andrew Carnegie's mother trying to buy a stove, suffering the salesman's dispensing of technical information about BTU's and heating coils and conductivity as long and as politely as she could but finally interrupting his lecture with: "what I want to know is – will this keep a little old lady like me warm in a drafty house?"… two, of the SILENT RAGE that must build up in many people, never voiced, as they are taught technical information when what they really want is to find a trustworthy person to sell them the stove that will keep them warm.

(*Napoleon Hill is most famous for the book, *Think And Grow Rich*, first published in 1937, still popular today, summarizing "laws of success" drawn from study of commonalities of hundreds of top achievers of his era – initiated at behest of Andrew Carnegie. Less well known, Hill was a successful advertising copywriter, then sales trainer, including tenure at W. Clement Stone's built-from-scratch giant life insurance sales organization that made Stone a billionaire. The company was ultimately sold to AEON.)

It is very important to understand your audience (prospect, client) – and what *THEY* want to know.

You think: the more you teach so the more they know, the more they trust. Nuts.

And don't think this is true merely of unsophisticated investors. It is even truer of affluent, successful, sophisticated people just like me – experts in what we do and very busy with it. I am not the least bit interested in learning about my investments or about financial planning or estate law or anything of the sort. **I am just as guilty and riddled with sinful sloth and dangerous irresponsibility about this as the next guy.** I sign forms attached to 50 page documents I never read. I do not comparison shop. My mind fuzzes over, then wanders out of the room when confronted with some detailed explanation of how this trust invests in this fund and the flibbergibbits are annualized and averaged and all I hear now is a faintly annoying buzz. And I'm worth many millions of dollars, only 55 and not yet addled, and work a lot with investment professionals and companies and even helped found a bank. But I am not interested in these details. I am interested in finding trustworthy people to simply tell me what I should do in my situation and then do it for me. After a point, the more you tell me, the less effective you are. You don't build trust, because I fear you're trying to baffle me with BS. You don't gain influence, because you lose my interest. *You annoy this pig.*

As evidence, let me give you some personal disclosures that should be embarrassing...

I have three classic cars and I have "a guy" at an auto repair company, who takes care of them. He comes and gets them, fixes this or that, tweaks this or that, gets whatever parts are needed, keeps them running as if new because I drive all three, and stores them in heated garages in winter. I get and pay invoices. I do not discuss costs in advance nor question charges after the fact. I trust him – and I do not want to be bothered. I'm not a "car guy" by the way. I can't even tell you what size motor is in the '72 Javelin AMX or the '65 Lincoln or the '86 Rolls. I just like driving them.

I have about a million dollars of apartment building and commercial real estate investments in Iowa. I invest in them sight unseen. I truthfully do not even understand all the tax ramifications – I have my CPA, who I trust, talk about that and work that out with my Iowa real estate guy, who I trust. Documents come with little "Sign Here" sticky-arrows on them, I sign them, return them and file copies. I would never invest in real estate if I had to give it ANY time or attention – my time is too valuable doing other things about which I am expert. I found a guy, Darin Garman, who I trust.

At our Ohio home, that I inhabit 90% of the time and my wife inhabits only about 50% of the time, there are things that need done. Storm doors off and patio furniture returned to the deck in Spring and vice versa in Fall, light bulbs replaced, pictures hung, a hinge fixed, etc., etc. – and for all these things we have "A Guy." He has a key to the house, so he can come and go as he sees fit, and can do most of this while we are out of town. At the end of each year, he gives me a bill for the year. It is a single amount written on a piece of paper. It includes whatever he's bought that was needed, his labor, his profit. It is

I Mentioned My Classic Cars...

This Rolls-Royce Corniche II was built for Dean Martin in 1986, until 1991, then in museums until I purchased it.

This is a rare 1972 AMC Javelin AMX with Pierre Cardin designer interior.

not itemized or supported with receipts. It is whatever it is. I am happy not to be bothered by these details, and I trust him to be fair.

Think I'm an idiot? You may be right. But there are a lot of me. I've had, in intimate, private coaching and mastermind group environments, over 20 or so years, over 200 millionaires, multi-millionaires and 7-figure earners, age 35 to 75. **They all ask each other and me where they should "put their money" – and, more importantly, *with whom*. They do not ask How It Works. They ask Who To Trust.**

This is VERY relevant to you – but not exclusively you. I teach it to chiropractors, dentists, veterinarians, consultants, carpet cleaners, home remodelers, auto shop owners, etc., etc. In all these cases, the majority of marketers focus on their What, but the majority of customers are focused on: Who? And they are not looking for a Teacher, to inform or educate them. They are looking for THE Person They Can Trust, to tell them what to do or do it for them.

I've even made my own verb for the right kind of marketing centered around this. I call it "WHO-ing." There is a science, a process, a collection of tools, procedures and practices for actively establishing yourself as *the* most trustworthy expert in a category, in the minds of a target group of prospects (which I teach in sophisticated detail in trainings for professional consultants, business coaches, doctors, attorneys, etc.). This is NOT to be confused with the ego-pandering "personal branding" quite often sold to those in your profession as a pricey package of fancy brochures and matching stationary with a clever slogan. Such tools have their place, and are arguably even essential, but they are merely tools in a toolbox – useless to an unskilled carpenter. WHO-ing encompasses foundational things like positioning; marketing science like precision targeting; tools as mentioned; and more, but is ultimately an active *behavioral* thing.

The bottom line is that there *are* certain things your clients want to know and want most, that, with your every word, gesture, piece of literature, they are trying to deduce and determine, consciously and subconsciously. There are also many things about what you do, and how you do it, and why you do it the way you do it, and how it is priced, and how it pays, that you think are important, and arguably should be important to your clients, that they have absolutely no interest in whatsoever, are intimidated by, made to feel dumb by, confused by, bored by, and even annoyed by. The pathway to a high-trust relationship is paved with what they want to know – not with what they should want to know or what you want them to know.

"To the client, salespeople all tend to look alike and blur together. They all ask the same questions, wear the same suits, make the same promises...<u>to stop being treated like a stereotypical salesperson, stop acting like one.</u> How does a stereotypical salesperson act? They try to convince, persuade, and sometimes manipulate. This is what sales-trainers have taught for 50 years...we need to stop talking about products and start talking to prospects about what is important to them. People buy for their reasons – not yours. At core, you are better advised to master the art of establishing trust, rather than 'sales techniques.' People buy from people they trust and respect. Then, you can stop trying to convince people to do business with you."

From: STEVE CLARK, author, *PROFITABLE PERSUASION: Put The Hay Down Where The Goats Can Get It*. Steve is one of the experts scheduled for exclusive interviews, in 2011, for a very select and limited number of advisors that are working with Matt Zagula and Advisors Excel.

CHAPTER 3
TRUST BUILT BY CONSISTENCY

BY MATT ZAGULA

McDonalds dominates the hamburger selling business why? Consistency. If you are down south in Naples, Florida and order a Big Mac it'll taste the same as the Big Mac you ate in Flint, Michigan. Is it the best tasting burger in town? No, but the customer knows what he or she is getting. There are no surprises with what they are served. The customer knows how it is going to taste, what the exterior of the building will look like and how their "meal" will be packaged—always done in a consistent way.

In many respects, consistency is the key ingredient in creating trust. So, my newspaper lead generation insert looks and says much of the same that is written about in my book, and discussed in my public seminars, and my staff and I use the same terminology, most of which we created, and the visuals all throughout my office all have a very consistent look, tone and message. Nothing will surprise a prospective client because there is a consistency to what we say, to what we do and how we show up—always in the same way, saying the same core values of our planning philosophy over and over—in print and in what we verbally say.

In my practice, we often integrate financial products with very specific trusts. Estate planning and elder law planning trusts really fall under three categories: irrevocable, revocable and a hybrid trust; commonly referred to as, a defective grantor trust. We are very careful to never mention any of these trusts because of the very dangerous possibility of being **Google Slapped!**

A little background on this crucially important matter, I tend to spend time with a lot of diverse professionals. A Google Slap to my online internet marketing friends means something totally different than what I want to discuss here with you; financial advisor to financial advisor.

Online a Google Slap has to do with how Google's algorithm changes and your site optimization falls. For the internet guys it's a hard blow because they work very hard to get "optimized" only to be slapped down by new Google rules. So, a slap to them costs them a lot of money.

That said, the Google Slap you and I can receive is every bit as expensive and costly. Let's talk about how Google, and the other search sites, hurt your business. Let's consider something very common and basic in our profession—Life Insurance:

Google

| life insurance | Search |

About 189,000,000 results (0.28 seconds)   **Advanced Search**

Sponsored links

1. **Life Insurance**

    www.SelectQuote.com   Speak to a Qualified Agent Today about Term **Life Insurance**.

2. Affordable **Life Insurance**

    www.ReliaQuote.com   Quickly Compare Term **Life** Rates. Rated "Best of the Web" by Forbes.

3. Affordable **Life Insurance**

    www.IntelliQuote.com   Want Affordable **Life Insurance**? Compare Rates & Apply Online Today!

    Get a Life Insurance Quote—Life Insurance 101—Contact Intelliquote Today

Search Results

1. **Life Insurance**, Dental Insurance & Financial Services | MetLife

As you can see, Google search offers the searcher 189 MILLION resources to review/study/ponder/consider and to "think about."

So, let's you and I "think about" a prospect in front of you who should buy life insurance. He gets out of the meeting telling you he needs to "think about it." He goes home, jumps on Google and searches life insurance and he goes to work. By the time your prospective client finishes his review of these 189 MILLION resources, articles and calculators he'll be dead. Obviously, beyond the point where the life insurance planning would have done him or his family any good.

Two Key Points:

1) Google is NOT your friend (nor is Yahoo, MSN, or the search engine your neighbor's 13-year-old kid is creating this week that will be the hit of 2011.)

2) The slap YOU get is YOUR own fault. Ouch, a self-inflicted wound.

Google creates this do-it-yourself 24/7 on-demand resource that is horrible for our prospects and clients, frankly. It's a self-inflicted wound because your selling process leads the client right to the point of "self-validation" of your concepts. This is where the mental disconnect happens for your prospect. Let me explain...

People, specifically your prospects, identify with certain terms, phrases and even single words. You must be very cautious of your words. Let's say the prospect hears you say the word trust, as in a Revocable Living Trust or an ILIT. They've heard that before so in their minds they want to do their due diligence, they want to validate your idea, for themselves, and be sure that your plan is good for them. In addition, they also want to make sure they are getting the best deal. Go ahead and Google "Life Insurance" and see how many of those millions of hits are about getting the best priced premium payment. No wonder retirees and those soon to be retired are stuck, like a deer in the headlights; it's just too much information available to them.

So, here's the fool-proof way to avoid the slap...

Write a list of common terms. Here's a quick partial list: mutual fund, annuity, life insurance, living trust, power of attorney, Irrevocable Trust (keep going with this). Then, simply, rename your planning process. Yep, it's that easy.

Sy Sperling did it for the toupee. He renamed the process "The Strand-By-Strand Hair System" for his hair replacement company, The Hair Club For Men. He changed the perception of an entire industry and ultimately sold the company for $210,000,000.00 to the Regis Company in 1976.

So, a secret to achieving greater success and the ultimate defense from the "think about it" prospect is to change the way the world looks at your planning process. In my office, we ALL call gifting and wealth transfer plans Protected Gift Accounts. Go ahead and Google that—you won't see much. Hey, by the way, don't go slapping that onto your website since I'm trying to help you here. Don't mess me up—okay—fair enough?

This in no way changes my firm's obligation to disclose details about the products and legal documents the client will ultimately receive. Full disclosure is always our professional and moral obligation. However, in the process of turning a prospect into a client you have no obligation to say certain words, phrases and terms that will lead them to Google. Your job, as a great advisor, is to help them cut through all the information and pick appropriate solutions to their most pressing financial and family planning problems. Part of that obligation is to hold their hands through the planning process...tightly...so their fingers don't type in www.google.com.

So, word consistency is just one example of how we develop trust with our prospects. In the process of becoming a client our message, our terminology and our appearance will remain steady and constant. This offers our soon-to-be new client peace of mind knowing that what he or she was attracted to was a core value and not that month's marketing pitch. Plus, our core message never changes so our clients can confidently refer to us knowing exactly how their referred friend will be treated.

This consistency is not limited to any specific financial discipline. Two of the best income planners in the business today are Chad and Bill,* both of whom have painstakingly charted out each component of their prospect's experience right up to the point of them becoming a new firm client. Bill and Chad teach newly recruited advisors at Advisors Excel how to set up their Registered Investment Advisory practice in a very logical way, taking into consideration the client's age and overall risk tolerance in a unique way, their proprietary model. Bill and Chad, both consulting clients of mine, are so driven by creating the perfect business model that these two seasoned, accomplished pros seek my counsel to stress test their ideas and processes seeking their ultimate business goal...Perfection!

* Last names withheld.

Almost all of the testimonials in this book come from consulting clients of mine who have completed my Total Market Domination® one-day intensive. In each case, these producers came to me already at the very tip top of our industry's production scale. These high achievers, of course, wanted more. They all walked away with a game plan to go farther, faster than they had ever gone before in a very compressed (short) period of time, all based on one key element, done in many different ways: attracting their perfect client, their Avatar, by creating a <u>consistent</u> message weaved through all of their marketing material, all of their client communication pieces, their office lobby appearance, their conference room décor and even how they dressed, spoke; all the way down to how they came in to greet their new prospect and their very first words.

Having all of this professionally manicured to please their perfect client visually and audibly creates instant peace of mind and once a person is at ease, their sales resistance goes down, allowing trust to quickly and permanently be gained.

CHAPTER 4

THE POWER OF EXCLUSIVITY

BY MATT ZAGULA

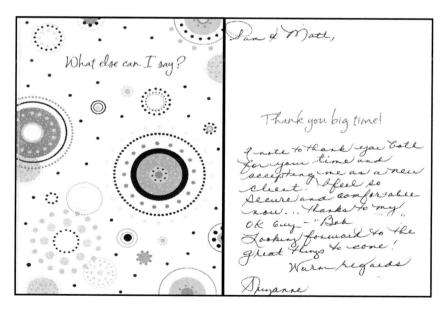

As you can see from the scanned images of the Thank You card we received from our new client Suzanne she is thrilled we **ACCEPTED** her as a new client. Now, I am guessing that terminology *accepted*, is quite foreign to financial advisors.

What Suzanne knew was that her friend Bob trusted us, he recommended us as her best option for safety and yield but warned her that we don't always accept new clients. This is powerful because it is 100% accurate—we don't take on everyone who comes to us with money and that positioning makes us much more magnetically attractive to our target prospective client.

Our firm, five years ago, adopted a new business philosophy after an intense study of how Dan Kennedy had coached cosmetic dentists and surgeons to position themselves. The best of these doctors in the country are ultra-exclusive and anyone, lucky enough to be walking through their door never asks how much it is going to cost. The "lucky ones" are just thrilled to be "IN." I immediately contrasted that business positioning to financial advisors; many of whom, get into their cars and drive to a prospective client's home on a Saturday morning leaving their own family to accommodate their prospect's schedule. With the typical result of: driving back home that beautiful Saturday morning to their kids waiting for their dad to go out to the park for the family picnic while those time vampires are supposedly "thinking over" what they offered.

So, let's dissect how we successfully, first, manufacture this level of exclusivity and how today, frankly, we *are* that exclusive.

First, we run a real business. We put into our market an attractive marketing message that attracts the prospects most likely to benefit, and therefore, invest in our offers. How? **We NEVER use bait and switch advertising. So, a FREE dinner or FREE lunch seminar is not an option for us because it positions us poorly.**

Does that ultra-exclusive surgeon in Beverly Hills have to buy prospective clients a dinner at Ruth Chris to fill his calendar with super wealthy clients? Hell no, and if he did it would freak out his existing clients and hurt his business. It would destroy his authority.

Next, we don't make it so easy for folks to get to us...

So, to get on our schedule you must either:

A) Come through a public workshop, agree to divulge your financial information, in advance, through our triage process and depending on your situation accept waiting three to six weeks for an appointment. If a prospect is unwilling to divulge financial information in advance they are respectfully told that they cannot come in because this is a part of our procedure and there's no flexibility.

OR

B) Be referred into our firm by one of the four "Blue Chip" Estate and/or Elder Law Practicing Law Firms. These firms are not here in my small town. In fact, a significant percentage of my business comes from Chicago, Illinois from the premier Elder Law Firm in that city. My lawyer referral source and friend, Rick Law, says it best: "we are our area's number one source for elder law services and our closest competitor is number four." It's true they are so dominant there's no number two or three to speak of...they own their market. Same is true of my referral sources from Overland Park, Kansas and the firm I work with in North Carolina—they are the entrenched leader. So, we only work with the best.

OR

C)   An A+ Client refers you "IN." Getting the thank you card above from Suzanne was awesome because she is as sweet of a client (of a person) as anyone of us could dream of BUT I may not have had that opportunity if it wasn't for Bob fully appreciating the value we bring and understanding the "social benefit" of getting Suzanne with us, as well as, his desire for his friend to get the best advice. He also got a Thank You card from Suzanne, fyi...

So Bob has this trust and confidence in us because we've always delivered on the promises we've made to him and he has been with us for several years. Suzanne respects Bob because he is accomplished in business and is a powerful success story. **Referrals are always strongest when they come from a person of power.** Bob is a known entrepreneur, a real life rags to riches story and a family man with a generous heart so people listen to him. Bob is a true Kennedy style "who" in our community—so our firm continues to grow because Bob benefits from being one of a very small group of clients we offer a golden key into our practice. If Bob refers the client is "IN," this gets us more clients like Bob, which is great because he is a perfect Avatar client, and Bob gets the recognition and he remains a powerful center of influence in our area's business community—so everyone involved benefits.

Keep in mind, none of this has anything to do with teaching our clients a lot of mind-numbing, intimidating and, to them, uninteresting information and investing, investment products and personal finance. Of course, we do that, to the extent necessary, and occasionally capitalize on a specific "money issue" in the news. But our practice is fueled by establishing trust, not by teaching.

Bob and Suzanne are products of a very strategic, sophisticated process for establishing trust that begins before someone gets to meet with us, all the way through their becoming a client, and beyond, for the continuation of the relationship. If you do not have this organized into your own systematic process and are, instead, relying simply on "doing a good job," on general client goodwill, you are settling for far, far less than you could be earning, and working harder than need be to convince clients to join you.

> "I know why the sun never sets on the British Empire. God would never trust an Englishman in the dark."

From: *THE BOOK OF INSULTS* – reflecting that being untrustworthy is an internationally recognized insult of great severity.

CHAPTER 5
A BIT OF INSIGHT INTO CLIENT CONTROL

BY DAN KENNEDY

In the previous Chapter, Matt gave glimpse at his process for controlling the new, prospective client's initial steps forward. The very idea of controlling the client (rather than eagerly responding to the client as the client asks) is very *s-t-r-a-n-g-e* to most advisors.

I do not believe in the "servant role." I believe clients all want a "stern but loving parent," and want to hand over control of their money to somebody who will relieve them of all their anxiety and worries about it. Business leaders want this when it comes to their advertising and marketing decisions and investments – once they trust me, they are eager for me to take this off their hands, do it or tell them what to do. I'm certain it's no different for the soon-to-retire or retired, modestly affluent boomer or senior. They don't want a subservient servant. They want a strong, authoritative, confident person in whom they can feel confident.

The "stern but loving parent" premise was passed to me about 25 years ago, by a prominent practice-management consultant in the chiropractic profession, Dr. Kirby Landis.

I also do not believe in gratitude as business strategy – either for client retention or referrals. I have very revealing stories about this and expensive lessons I've been taught about it, that this book lacks room for. But I want to give you a quote from a book titled *Lost Secrets of Fame and Fortune:*

> **The wise man would rather see men needing him than thanking him. To keep them on the threshold of hope is diplomatic (productive), to trust to their gratitude, foolish. Hope has a good memory, gratitude a bad one. More is to be got from dependence than courtesy. Remember, he that has satisfied his thirst turns his back on the well.**

Does that strike you as cynical? How you feel about it shouldn't matter, from a business strategy standpoint. It is sound caution about human nature. The man who built one of the most amazing "human potential movement" companies, which you've probably heard of – EST – understood this. I once privately asked Werner Erhard to succinctly explain how EST functioned from a business and financial standpoint, not a philosophical one. He said: "We preach independence but breed dependence." In short, trust is not at all enhanced by transfer of knowledge and capability from you to clients. They are not interested in becoming expert about finances and investing. They are interested in finding a trustworthy expert. While they would never enunciate a desire for dependence rather than independence, that is, in fact, exactly what they're after – safe, secure dependence.

Only about 1% to no more than 5% of any gathered population or of society in general has ambition for independence, autonomy and control – with it comes enormous personal responsibility. If you are in that elite group, which you may very well be, congratulations. But don't plan on making a living on such clients. They are too few and not particularly needy. Instead, you will do well to create high-trust relationships with people possessing significant investable assets, who are eager to find someone to make their money, investment and security decisions for them.

So, finally, I will try to succinctly summarize what clients secretly want from a financial advisor. If you make everything you say, do, present, deliver about this, clients will gladly hand over control to you and stay with you forever. This means, incidentally, that learning more and more, going deeper and deeper, and getting evermore sophisticated about this (as opposed to, say, product knowledge or financial machinations or even conventional selling skills) should be your prime interest, your fascination, your intellectual hobby. Here it is. **What they want, above all else...**

Wait, one minute more. Let me list a few things people in your field might think is this thing – but is incorrect. Highest or best yield. No. Brand-name. No. Best ratings by independent agencies. No. Clever, creative investment products. No. Knowledge. As I've said, no. These things and others like them can certainly factor into someone's buying decision, but only when presented in context, and as evidence of and support for the thing they really want. And too much emphasis on any of these things can actually obscure what they really want.

So, what they want, above all else, is…

Peace of mind.

In his infomercial, where master pitchman Ron Popeil sells his countertop rotisserie grill, he repeats a line again and again, a little rhyme: *you just set it and forget it.* He knows. With more complex purchases, most still want to just set it and forget it. They want you to be in control. They draw confidence and comfort from the advisor who is clearly in control of his own business and life, in control of his client relationships, in control of his investment methodology. My speaking colleague of 9 years, Zig Ziglar, describes successful selling as *transference of feeling* (not transfer of knowledge). The sense that the advisor is firmly in control is a feeling that fosters trust.

If you will educate, train and condition yourself to be a master salesman of Peace of Mind (rather than of anything else, including financial products or plans), you will prosper as never before.

CHAPTER 6
CLIENTS BROUGHT TO YOU

BY DAN KENNEDY

Brought to you. Not just told about you. Not just referred to you. *Brought to you.*

How do you know if you are trusted? How can we objectively measure your success at creating trust with your clients? The harsh reality is revealed by your referrals. I first heard about the "endless chain of referrals" from Paul J. Meyer, a famously successful insurance company developer, who went on to create Success Motivation Institute and its flagship home study course Dynamics of Personal Achievement. Paul's premise was that you never needed to be without a good prospect as soon as you had just one client, unless you were inept at trust. *Every* client should beget another. I grasped it, and made the concept a major part of my own business approach. In my own professional practice as a business advisor and direct-response copywriter, I have an 85%+ repeat/reoccurring patronage factor and nearly that high a referral factor – unheard of in my industry, unimaginable to my peers. This is the accurate reflection of my efficacy at establishing trust. When a client sends one of their friends or colleagues to me, they know that person will likely be "risking" upwards from $100,000.00 on my advice and services, and that if the person they referred has an unsatisfactory experience, they *will* hear about it. Thus, they "risk" when referring.

You need to truthfully assess your efficacy at trust, stated as fact by the percentage of your clients who bring clients to you.

You won't like the comparison, but the most successful High Trust Salesperson I've ever known – and often took customers to – was a car salesman in Phoenix. For sake of this short chapter, I'm not going to tell you the whole story; it's on page 65 of my book, *No B.S. Sales Success In The New Economy*, if you're curious. I'll just tell you the pay-off. This guy stayed #1 at the biggest Ford dealership in the Southwest for many consecutive years because he had large numbers of customers *insisting* their spouses, other family members, friends and co-workers go to him when ready to buy a car, often actually calling to make the appointment for the person, loading the person in their car, and taking him to the appointment and tagging along throughout, making sure the family member or friend didn't embarrass them by questioning price or otherwise displaying any rude resistance and was properly respectful and appreciative. I did this myself with wife, parents, brothers, two business associates. Consequently, incidentally, nearly 100% of these dozens of brought-to-him appointments each month resulted in immediate sales, and price rarely challenged let alone negotiated. In a business where it is universal knowledge you're supposed to haggle over price.

As a car salesman, this guy had a pretty cushy existence. Not by accident, but not from constant or even frequent overt asking for referrals. He was so low-key about that it felt *sleepy*. This happy situation was product of High Trust Selling and being a High Trust Sales Professional.

Most salespeople don't get this at all. They think they do. They give lots of lip service to it. But they still think of trust in terms of a necessary tool for making sales. They don't think of it as THE objective of all they do. Personally, I have, on numerous occasions, refused to take offered money from somebody eager to retain me and eager for certain services, and refused to make that sale, instead choosing to end with trust rather than fee. In some cases, this has sub-sequently led to subsequent acceptance of my recommendations. In other cases, the word has gone back from the surprised, gently refused would-be client to the person who sent him to me, greatly strength-ening that referror's trust in me, and subsequently leading to more referrals of more appropriate clients. In other cases, the word has just gotten around and reinforced something I very much want known about me: that I do not accept just anybody as a client, and I don't work or write to assignment. I'm in charge.

In my business, well over half of my private clients are brought to me by others. As example, in late summer 2010, a freelance copywriter who knows me and has attended my seminars *asked permission (!)* to bring one of her biggest clients to me, for consulting about his pub-lishing business, growing thanks to her efforts, but still not exploiting some of its best opportunities. Granted such permission, she gave him all the "rules of the road" and made sure he behaved himself properly, so when he did contact my assistant, he took one of the three choices of days offered him, booked his day at $18,800.00, Federal Expressed in his 50% deposit, and will, I assure you, be sure to have his materials in the seven business days beforehand required, will be at the local hotel specified, ready to be picked up at 8:30A.M. on the morning three months hence, and will be a model client that day. It's likely there will be six-figures in fees and royalties for me as a result of that day. I will not even speak with him before that day. There was not the usual-in-the-consulting-business requests for client references that can be called, the plethora of questions in advance before deciding to book the advice day, any adverse reaction to fee, none of that. Because he was *brought.*

You may be able to let yourself off this hook by saying, "Well, I'm not Dan Kennedy." But surely you can't insist you are inferior to a car salesman.

If you do not have clients bringing you good clients, and a number of clients repeatedly bringing you new clients, you won't like hearing this but: *you are failing.* There's something very wrong. You should be beneficiary of what I first learned about from Paul J. Meyer: the endless chain of referrals. You should be beneficiary of the Rule of 52*, which I invert to 25. The rule is: on average, everybody knows 52 people important enough in their lives to at least notify, if not invite to a wedding or funeral – half live locally. Because birds of feather do flock together, at least half of those have much in common in age, income, financial status, needs, etc., so if every client hasn't brought you a dozen, *you are failing.* And the "spread" between your reality i.e. number of direct, brought to you referrals per client and that potential number is accurate measurement of how well you are doing or how badly you are failing. Don't BS yourself or me with yakkity-yak about how beloved and trusted you are by your clients: this number tells the truth.

The good news is: your number can be substantially improved by altering about five simple things in the way you conduct your business, most of which are quite painless. These five fixes are things I teach within the context of High Trust Status***. They are very straightforward, practical to-do's. But here, at least consider the foundational premise: stop trying to make sales and focus instead, as "job #1," on achieving High Trust Status with everyone you interact with. It changes *everything*.

By the way, there are plenty of specific referral stimulation strategies I provide to professionals – but none of them work well when, in reality, the minimum level of trust is present, and they all work infinitely better when high trust is present.

I'll close with one other secret few professionals or business owners understand: it requires a great deal more trust to refer to you than it does just to do business with you and invest with you. Championing someone to family, friends, peers bears much, much, much greater emotional risk than does giving you my money. You can even successfully sell with low trust, but you won't see people sold with low trust bringing you additional clients. If you'd love a referral-driven career, this is key.

* The Rule of 52 comes from Joe Girard, in the *Guinness Book of World Records* for many years as America's #1 Salesman. ***This training is provided via a particular seminar, coaching program and special resources made available exclusively via Matt Zagula and Advisors Excel. For information, visit: **www.MATTZAGULA.com/AE**

CHAPTER 7
TRUST BUILT OR DAMAGED BY DEMONSTRATION

BY DAN KENNEDY

I have a great deal to say about Demonstration. When I conduct high-level seminars for consultants, coaches, professionals – like doctors and attorneys, and entrepreneurs I often show newsreels of Houdini's escapes, a segment from "The Pitchmen" television show, and other demonstrations of the power of Demonstration. It is Wealth-Magnet #11 in my book, *No B.S. Wealth Attraction for Entrepreneurs.* It is put in context of Sales Choreography® in the *Uncensored Sales Strategies* book I co-authored with Sydney Barrows, the former, once-infamous 'Mayflower Madam'. With private clients, I often guide them to incorporating Demonstration in their marketing and selling.

Demonstration is, essentially, a form of visual proof – typically, dramatic. Whatever it is you want to prove, you figure out a way to demonstrate its truth. This can be as abbreviated as the soaking up of a gallon of spilled Coca-Cola® with the "magic shammy cloth" in a 60-second TV commercial, or something much broader; in my case,

I strive to provide my readers, newsletter subscribers, Glazer-Kennedy Insider's Circle™ Members, etc. with continuing demonstration of the core principles I teach and champion to them.

My life is my Demonstration. I don't need to enunciate it or connect the dots for those viewing it and hearing about it; it is self-evident. For example, I guide businesspeople to Autonomy. That is, working how you want, when you want, with whom you want, at the price/fee you want. I do not own or use and therefore am not tethered to or controlled by a cell-phone, I do not therefore text or tweet or receive such intrusions, I do not use e-mail; access to me is carefully controlled and rationed, all of which is explained in my book, *No B.S. Time Management for Entrepreneurs*, and explained to private clients at the very start if it is not already known to them. I take care of every necessary phone conversation for the month in one to no more than two days during the month, via pre-scheduled appointments with start and end times. I own about 20 harness racehorses and even drive myself professionally about 200 times a year, making it important to be the home by the track most Monday, Tuesday, Wednesday and Saturday nights, so I make clients and groups come to me and I travel on business rarely and grudgingly. Racehorses, by the way, are the proverbial worst known investments – they eat while I sleep, and they come with veterinarians who have kids going to college attached. I have, now, three classic cars which I also use in my self-marketing, and make the points of income-at-will and sending-the-bill-to-the-herd with them.

Immediately, of course, you will think I'm lying about the way I do business and govern the way people do business with me, but as you get to know me you'll determine for yourself it's real. You'll also think I can but you can't, and your clients would never and you must be at instant beck 'n call, but with time, I'll convince you otherwise and liberate you from the tyranny. But that's another conversation for another time. Here, now, I just use the Demonstration of Autonomy as an example of how I use Demonstration. It is part and parcel of getting people intrigued, curious and curiouser, interested, fascinated with me (and if you haven't yet read the book *FASCINATE* by Sally Hogshead you should).

Now, why is all this so important to you?

Two reasons – one nearly unique to you; that one first. You are more actually restricted in using testimonials and more timid about finding legal ways to use them than just about any other profession or business. An essential form of proof is denied you. Worse, certain competitors for your clients' attention, interest and investment dollars are free to use them, and do. "Social proof" is a driver of trust far more powerful, when properly used, than any other. My private clients, combined, sold over $4-billion in goods and services last year; the companies directly attached to me alone, some $30-million…and not a dollar of it was independent from social proof, and much of it was the direct return on extensive investment in use of it. Anybody who knows anything about direct marketing will confirm for you: **you are at extreme disadvantage in the trust game, deprived of this. You might as well be an NFL team deprived of a quarterback, having to put the halfback in that position, and use only running plays – never a pass. Or play against Tiger and Phil in the PGA Tournament with only a putter and wedge – no driver.**

There are peers of mine; advertising, marketing, direct marketing specialists, strategists and copywriters who have told me they have avoided anything to do with regulated financial services providers because they view this as too heavy a handicap.

The reason why social proof used smartly is so powerful is simply that what others like me say about you to me is infinitely more believable than what you say about you – even if you are infinitely more eloquent. I own racehorses. When a salesman comes to the barn and pitches us on some new nutritional supplement, laser treatment device or other gadget, etc., we are markedly uninterested in what he has to say. We are very interested in what one of the top trainers in the country or just another trainer we know well, a respected peer, especially a grizzled veteran skeptical of everything new has to say about it. The salesman labors under burden of distrust: we know his agenda and purpose, we expect him to only extol virtues and hide flaws, we assume exaggeration, we know he's not one of us – he does not own, train or race horses. Our buddy who knows much about training and conditioning horses is granted benefit of trust. (By the way, THE last thing you can afford being pigeon-holed as is "another salesman". See: Chapter 9.)

So, you are at extreme, extreme, extreme disadvantage, when real limits plus self-imposed limits prohibit you from using the #1 driver of trust.

It's not particularly productive or profitable to cry about that. You need to be inspired and motivated to action by this adversity. This means you (a) must be far, far, far better at everything else to compensate for your handicap and (b) you must find and use substitutes for social proof. One such substitute is effective Demonstration.

I have 12 different Demonstrations for trustworthiness, and you have opportunities to use them all. Since this is candidly an introductory, get-acquainted and starting-point book and not an exhaustive training, I'll give you two – the two easiest, simplest, pretty much obvious ones, yet ones poorly used by most.

One is **absolute punctuality.** The more affluent and experienced the person you're dealing with, the more likely it is he shares my own litmus test: if you can't keep small commitments, you damn sure can't be trusted to keep big ones. Also, the older your client, the more likely it is that he values largely by-gone standards of civilized and professional behavior, and that includes punctuality. I happen to have a personal fetish for it, so it's not been that difficult for me to discipline myself, but for others it is extremely difficult – which is all the more reason to master it. In my own professional practice, clients need to know they can trust me to meet deadlines, or to be where I'm supposed to be ready to perform, and to function without need for their micro-management, cajoling or baby-sitting. One of the ways I use to dem-onstrate discipline is by operating via pre-set phone appointments and then, if it is for 9:20 A.M., I am on the phone at 9:19 A.M., and if it is to end at 9:40, even if we are in mid-sentence, I end it at 9:40 because I have – and they know I have—another call to start at 9:40. A statement is made by my behavior.

The other is **follow-up.** Many things factor into follow-up. I'll just talk about one here: the dichotomy between the prospect's or client's clock and yours. Let's say someone has responded to an ad, mailing, etc. and requested your free report on the *19 Secret Evils of Health Care Reform and How They May Rob You & Your Loved Ones of Financial Security*, or some such thing. You get that request on a Monday. To you, it seems perfectly reasonable to accumulate those requests during the week and have your secretary send out all the packets by mail on Thursday. This means that prospect will get it the following Tuesday – *just* 8 days from the time he asked for it. But when did he *want* it?

When he called or filled out and mailed in the form or provided info on the web site. If online, you could automate instant fulfillment of an e-version, but that would be a big mistake for a number of reasons I won't discuss here. So, let's assume he was "in heat" about this on Monday, September 6 and it arrives on Tuesday, September 14. What impression does that convey to him *about you?* Sorry, but the answer is: slow and unresponsive and disappointing which translates in his subconscious to: untrustworthy. Now assume he asked for it on Monday, it was FedEx'd on Monday and arrived Tuesday. What impression does that convey? Well, it risks conveying unbusyness and desperation, but that is easily fixed with the reasons for overnight delivery you give in your letter in the package. Then, it conveys that "hey, this guy is on the ball", responsive, to be trusted. This is even more critical when a Promise Is Made, because your would-be client is wondering if Promises Made Will Be Promises Kept. So even the casual conversation, in which you take somebody's business card and promise to send him a copy of your book is not really casual at all. If you "get 'round to it" a week or two later, you have muffed an opportunity to create trust and may have earned distrust demerits. If that book arrives the next day or day after, with Post-It Notes on pages related to your conversation, and a personal note, you have capitalized on an opportunity to create trust.

In my world, by the way, we work on four kinds of Follow-Up, on unconverted leads – foolishly, slothfully wasted by most, on new clients, on existent clients and on centers of influence…all incorporated in what I call a "NO-FAIL FOLLOW-UP SYSTEM." The four kinds are:

1: Personal-Relevance Follow-Up

2: Consistent, Discipline-Demonstration Follow-Up

3: Frequent Follow-Up

4: Persistent Follow-Up

In terms of content, by the way, I work to constantly reinforce positioning from this Pyramid of Power & Income (Shown, page 63).

But the point for here and now is that Punctuality and Follow-Up are two (of twelve) worthy means of Demonstration Of Trustworthiness that can either serve you well and help compensate for your heavy handicap (prohibiting effective use of social proof) or work against you, silently and secretively, possibly never voiced to you by anybody as reason they're not doing business with you but doing damage nonetheless, like an undiagnosed cancer.

Incidentally, in seminar, when I talk about Trust-Building By Demonstration, I usually show some old black-and-white newsreels of Houdini's biggest stunts, video clips from TV's most successful "pitchmen," and other actual demonstrations of the use of dramatic demonstration – and I promise you, there are hidden, powerful tactics YOU can borrow from such examples.

Here is the full-bore challenge of Demonstration: make a list of a half-dozen to a dozen things you need or want prospective clients and clients to believe as fact and know about you, that will contribute to their having a high level of trust in you. Make the items on that list as specific as possible. Not vague – like "I care about my clients' goals" or "I'm a good guy." With your list, think, think, think some more… get expert coaching to assist you…brainstorm with qualified cohorts…

search outside your industry for ideas…until you develop as many ways as possible to use Demonstration for each of those key things you want known about you.

RESOURCES NOTE: In 2009, taking effect beginning in 2010, new FTC rules took effect restricting the ways testimonials and other social proof could be safely used by advertisers of many different products and services, and this new rulebook adversely affected many of my clients. I went to work on their behalf and developed an entire "toolbox" I call: HOW TO PROVE YOUR CASE WITHOUT WITNESSES. This has evolved to a Module of training I am including in the Advanced Client Attraction, Conversion And Control Seminar for Financial Advisors that my co-author, Matt Zagula conducts, where I am there as a guest speaker, and that I provide via Matt's special coaching program exclusively for elite, top-performing advisors associated with ADVISORS EXCEL. If you'd like a 3-page Briefing about "Proving Your Case Without Witnesses," it will be faxed to you on request, by fax to 602-269-3113, no cost, no obligation.

HIERARCHY PYRAMID OF INCOME AND POWER

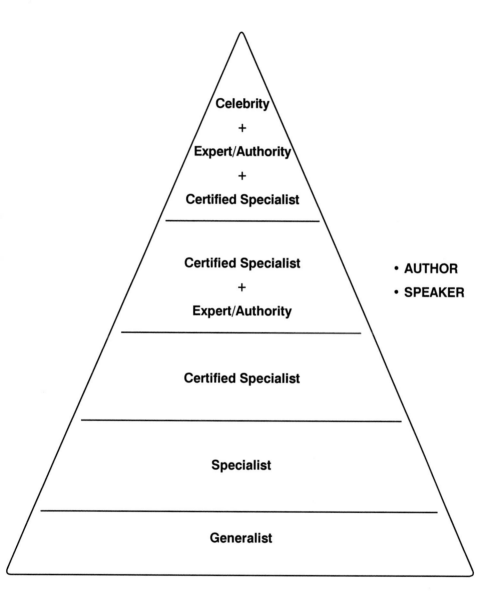

Celebrity
+
Expert/Authority
+
Certified Specialist

Certified Specialist
+
Expert/Authority

• AUTHOR
• SPEAKER

Certified Specialist

Specialist

Generalist

CHAPTER 8

SHOW UP LIKE NO ONE ELSE AND TOTALLY DOMINATE YOUR MARKET

BY MATT ZAGULA

Advisors can gain great differentiation from their competition by mastering the skills of demonstration. This advantage can be gained in two distinct ways: First, the advisor's ability to illustrate the complex in a way that simplifies the concept and gets to the core value of "doing the deal." Next, is to harness any third party credibility available that validates you are trustworthy and exceptional at your profession. Traditionally, the third party credibility is best accomplished by the testimonial of current clients who are screaming fans of yours. Unfortunately, that is not compliant.

So, first let's tackle the third party credibility issue head on in a world where we, as financial advisors, just cannot use testimonials. The first consulting client I worked with on this was Coach Pete*. Coach Pete is a well known advisor in North Carolina primarily because of the success of Coach Pete Radio. Pete has successfully branded himself as the voice of financial sanity in his area and in other key markets around the country with other advisors he helps to produce local market Coach Pete shows for lead generation purposes, quite successfully.

*Last name withheld.

Pete retained my services so that I could help him amplify his message through my Total Market Domination® process. A Big hurdle for Pete was not being allowed to get his numerous clients to sing his praises. With the regulatory environment as it is today, he felt it was risky when his client, unsolicited to do so, would call into his radio show and want to tell the listeners how much they trusted and appreciated Pete's work. Imagine somebody telling the truth about you, praising you and in the end getting you a regulatory slap—that's our world...sad.

So, a closely guarded secret to creating trust is what I call 'Saint marketing.' In Pete's case it was the Saint Pete plan. You see, Pete had charities in North Carolina that he truly supported. From memory, Pete's charities of choice were the Jimmy V Foundation and the Wounded Warrior—both great causes.

The plan was to incorporate charity into Pete's marketing. His Total Market Domination® consultation led us to the creation of a unique Shock And Awe Package*. This, a package that could be sent to Pete's listeners so they could get to know Pete and his core philosophy about money management before they came to see Pete. Don't confuse a marketing brochure with a Shock And Awe Package. His Shock And Awe Package contains pre-recorded, the best of Pete, radio shows, his most recent book and two DVDs. One of the DVDs was his recent interview for a 30 minute TV show where he was acknowledged as a Leading Expert in the area of finance and investing (technically, an infomercial for his services). The second DVD was the Saint Pete piece.

*I first heard this terminology—Shock And Awe Package—from Dan Kennedy, who has developed these to the highest level, in many professions and business fields.

For the Saint Pete piece we scripted out an event where Pete would bring in the charities mentioned above and make a significant donation to them to help them with their very important cause. Pete would speak briefly and explain that the community has done so much for him, for his family, his employees and his business that this is a way for him to give back to help people in his community in need and that he is honored to help. Then we would have the leaders from the organizations, holding Pete's check, say that without help from people like Pete they wouldn't be able to help families who rely on them and that it's generosity like his that keeps them going.

Now, this is all about truly helping the charity, it's a real check and it has to be significant enough to them to make an impact and to attend this event. Charities, nationwide, have been devastated by the economic turmoil and donations are down. So, they would welcome any idea that provides them with money.

Because of compliance we just can't do testimonials. But how powerful of a demonstration of credibility is it to have a charity leader standing there saying you help people in need who are fighting cancer, soldiers who are financially in need because of injuries and perhaps a third charity that cares for unwanted animals? The mind of the viewer screams out: "hey, this has to be a great guy...a *trustworthy* guy—right?" Unfortunately, this is a powerful tool to building significant trust quickly and bad people have exploited it, but for you, the reputable advisor, this is a wonderful way to gain powerful third party credibility in a compliant way. Just like Pete did (who is a world class advisor).

Another demonstration device: I've long been a raving fan of the whiteboard. In fact, I have a whiteboard in just about every room in my office building. There is power in being able to draw illustrations, while standing up in front of your prospects and clients, that explain planning techniques in an easy to understand way that motivates prospects to do business with you. Drawing these examples "spontaneously" is a much more powerful demonstration than using pre-done power points slides or literature.

Another consulting client of mine, Chris*, does this exceptionally well. Chris, recently, was named one of the five most influential senior advisors in America and was considered for *Senior Advisor* Magazine's Senior Advisor of the Year. He uses visualization to illustrate financial problems on his conference room whiteboard, then uses very simplistic diagrams to chart "potential" solutions and then offers the client the opportunity to get specific recommendations by paying his planning fee.

* Last name withheld.

Thanks to his mastery of explaining the complex, or as he explains it: "the money falling through the cracks" with compelling visual displays he commands an advanced fee to get his planning recommendations where other advisors in his market are just happy to get to "pitch" their plan. Chris, through powerful imagery, commands an advanced fee before offering his solutions which include managed money, life insurance and safe money annuity based solutions.

So, a great way to build trust in an untrusting world is to visually simplify the complex and offer solutions with straight talk, not double talk. Be careful to keep it on a level the client is comfortable on and never talk down to anyone because that's an instant turn off. Don't try to impress the higher net worth crowd with fancy lingo and industry jargon...keep it simple and sell a lot more—like Chris does.

Then, add in the power of being a good charitable person—be that saint and live up to it. Helping people has a multiplication affect on wealth—you truly can give and grow rich. Take that secret from me, help people in need and reap the benefits of being a trustworthy, community focused business owner—the ROI here is big!

ABOUT TRUST AND PERSONALITY

"...shy or low-key personalities can be as fascinating as the most charismatic ones, especially if they trigger trust. TRUST IS THE MOST POWERFUL TRIGGER IN RELATIONSHIPS...the need is not for one personality type to transform into another, but rather to maximize existing strengths and remove barriers to communication."

ABOUT TRUST AND CONSISTENCY

"...you can dabble in Prestige or experiment with Power, but you can't dip in and out of trust. It must be ESTABLISHED CONSISTENTLY. ...earning trust demands an investment of time and effort. Trusted brands (professionals) carefully pay attention to detail, reinforcing consistency between expectations they set and results they deliver."

From: *FASCINATE* (7 Triggers to Persuasion and Captivation) by Sally Hogshead. Sally and her work have been featured in *The New York Times* and on *The Today Show*, she has delivered keynotes on her subjects for leading companies like Microsoft and Starbucks, and consults with Fortune 500 companies on creating more fascinating products and advertising. **Sally is one of the experts scheduled for exclusive interviews, in 2011, for members of Matt Zagula's elite coaching program for select Advisors Excel's advisors.**

CHAPTER 9
ANOTHER SALESMAN

BY DAN KENNEDY

The last thing you want to be (perceived as) is: another salesman.

Sorry, but salesmen are not held in very high regard – even by other salesman. Yet, everybody who succeeds in just about any field is, in actuality, a salesman – my exclusive interview with Dr. Roizen of the Cleveland Clinic, as seen on *Oprah*, and co-author of the bestselling series of *YOU* books reveals much about this. (Reprinted at the end of this Chapter.) **Every successful person is a successful salesperson, but the most successful people are never thought of as salesmen.**

I have, for example, as a long-time private coaching client, one of the most successful, highest-fee cosmetic dentists in the eastern half of the United States, with per-case fees ranging from $40,000.00 to $70,000.00 and up, and over an 80% success rate at converting prospects to patients. Everything that occurs between the time a new, prospective patient raises his hand and that appointment, the person's experience from arrival at the office, and the case presentation itself is strategically planned, choreographed, scripted, and the doctor is a consummate professional salesperson…but I assure you, none of these patients think of him as such. Another long-time private coaching client of mine owns an upscale, high-priced martial arts academy in Louisiana. His fees are double his close competitors. His revenues and profits grew from '08 to '09 and from '09 to '10. He has over an 80% success rate in his sales presentation appointments with new, prospective clients. He is a consummate salesman, but I assure you, none of his clients think of him as such. These are typical of individuals I work with, who personally earn 7-figure yearly incomes.

These individuals' 80%+ "closing rates" are unheard of in their fields – just as it is in yours. In yours, working with pre-qualified prospects brought to appointments after seminars or through advertising, even top income financial advisors close fewer than 60%, and the average advisor half *that!* This is, in my opinion, deplorable. And fixable. Of course, you have to admit you have a problem before you can solve it. Get real about what your closing percentage is. Determine to make it better.

I am a fan and student of magic. Magic is about three things: what is seen, what is absolutely and clearly able to be seen but is never noticed, and what is unseen. The third is the least important, and is rather mundane. The first is performance style, and it varies a lot from one top magician to another. Chris Angel, for example, has a very different style than, say, Copperfield, and both vary greatly from Penn & Teller. In the same way, you can have a different style than Matt or some other top-performing, 7-figure income advisor and both of you can be successful. But that second component – that which is able to be seen but goes unnoticed, unseen, not perceived as what it is – is the most intriguing, difficult and important aspect of magic. And of being a consummate sales professional utilizing the most effective sales, persuasion and influence techniques and actually selling products and services yet not being perceived as a salesman or as someone selling.

As an aside, what psychics do – called "cold reading" – is extremely useful for financial advisors to understand and utilize, and there are even script templates for doing it.

Anyway, the point is, if they see, smell or sense "salesman selling," trust becomes nearly unobtainable. When the polar opposite is achieved, trust becomes virtually automatic.

The Failures Of Medicine / The Selling Of Concepts

Exclusive, In-Person Interview, Dan Kennedy with Dr. Michael Roizen M.D.

DSK: Many seeing the bestselling books in the 'You' series, beginning with *You: The Owner's Manual*, the PBS specials on TV, and knowing of the online business RealAge.com would be surprised to find you still in private practice. They might view the process of becoming a successful author and entrepreneur as distinctly apart from practice. Others will think what you've done beyond them at any level. I wanted to talk with you to introduce professionals to this path, perhaps not on a national level, but at least in their own market areas, of creating something unique to them, of becoming a recognized authority and celebrity because of it. It does take something of an entrepreneurial mindset. So **let me start by asking if you had to make a big switch here, from thinking like and being a doctor to being an entrepreneur?**

DR. ROIZEN: I never switched. I believe and continue to believe my strength is in communicating with patients. That just expanded from one on one to one to many. What I developed was for my practice, a way to motivate patients. (The RealAge metrics and presentations.) We found patients not just motivated by it with regard to their health, but a number of them with business backgrounds encouraged me and offered to assist me in taking it beyond the practice. They really started the process of commercializing it. The process of writing about it, and writing about it in a way that was appealing and motivating was an extension of what I did every day in the practice. I look at it, that I have two full-time jobs, one is as physician; the other is, **selling the public on getting healthy.** So, for anyone to follow my path, I think you have to be good enough in delivering medical care (or delivering your professional services), and then **be highly skilled at selling your patients (clients) on doing what they need to do** – whether it's actually doing the exercises you need to do, to prevent reoccurring neck and back pain, or making the right food choices – we are constantly selling patients. **Then, then, you're ready to talk to the public** effectively and persuasively just as if you are talking to that one patient. That's what I brought forward.

DSK: To be simplistic in summary, I would say that you've broken your business down into three parts: clinical, public relations, and the business aspects, and it's significant that you retained public relations for yourself. In fact, it is my observation over 30 years that THE difference between extraordinarily successful practitioners, including those who expand beyond practice and those who do not, vs. the majority of practitioners with modest, average or below-average incomes is to be found in the way the patients are motivated, reflected in how many people they talk positively and even persuasively to about their experience, and in how prominent the doctor is in his community, in the media and otherwise, through his deliberate and active effort at selling and promoting himself. That connects directly to the doctor's attitudes about selling. This may interest you: in an admittedly informal survey I've done of chiropractors and dentists, virtually all of them I've met with very high 6-figure or 7-figure incomes had sales experience in their youth, while working their way through college...they sold in homes, things like cookware, encyclopedias, fire alarms, or sold insurance, or worked in retail environments selling, and got good at it. Conversely, almost every practitioner I've ever known who consistently struggles in practice and struggles financially lacks that experience. I can tell you a lot about a doctor just by seeing if the bookshelves in his private office contain books about selling or not. **Just now, you used the word "selling" – three times – with no cringe.**

I'm sure you know, most doctors cringe at the word. Most visibly. Almost all internally. The word conjures mental pictures and represents a role they are not comfortable with. Some view it as unprofessional. When talking with them, most people who do what I do dance around it, say "case presentation" instead of "sales presentation" for example. You do not. Why are you so comfortable with describing what you do as selling?

DR. ROIZEN: I think that **the failure of medicine**, the failure to get adherence with what we suggest is because we think as M.D.'s we are deities, because we wear The White Coat that patients will do what we say. That's one of the great failures of medicine. Even if the pills are free, in the V.A., and patients who have hypertension and know that it is a serious disease, only 1/3rd of those patients take the pills as prescribed – and that's when the pills are free! Only 2/3rds even fill the prescription to start with. So **our failure in medicine is failing to understand that we have to sell health,** and then making ourselves expert and proficient at that. Just *telling* a patient is not enough, if you don't get into the emotions of that individual, if you can't get that patient to really understand why it's important for them. So, to come back to the question, selling is what we must do. If we don't sell, we don't get patients healthy. **The reason that my entire business outside the practice works as well as it does is that I am able to sell my concepts.**

DSK: That last thing you said is extremely important, because most doctors find it very awkward and difficult to publicly promote themselves, even to create a lot of word of mouth marketing from within, because they are selling themselves. They get a cold shoulder from the media because no media is eager to give free advertising to anybody, so trying to get interviewed to talk about a business, a practice, is nearly impossible. **What you did for yourself, the basis of everything, was invent interesting concepts to talk about – with patients, with the public and**

with the media. Doctors reading this should thoroughly look at your RealAge concepts, presented at RealAge.com and in the original Real Age books to understand this. The point is very important. It's not so much about selling yourself or selling how great your practice is, or selling medicine like a salesman sells products from a sample case. **It's about creating a unique concept that's interesting to talk about, arouses curiosity – in your case, well, what is my real age? In my work, I talk about going into a marketplace as either an annoying pest or a welcome guest. You get to be a welcome guest by bringing forward concepts that people are instantly interested in and want to know more about.** I've also taught this in terms of securing permission to sell; when you answer the "What do you do?" or "what business are you in?" question, does the person immediately, enthusiastically say "Really? Tell me more?" Obviously, if you say "I'm a doctor" or "I'm a dentist," that kind of eagerness to hear all about what you're all about isn't often forthcoming. But if you say something like "I have a unique, patented system for revealing what a person's real age is, and telling them exactly how they could feel and basically be 10 or 15 years younger," then that kind of response is there, and the welcome mat is out in front of just about every door. **That, to me, is the genius of what you've done – but it is a duplicatable genius.** Anybody can delve into their own knowledge, expertise, interests, passions, what they do, how they work with patients and develop their own proprietary concept. You did it a second time with the *You: An Owner's Manual* idea.

In marketing, we talk about such things as Unique Selling Proposition (USP), Unique Value Proposition (UVP), positioning, differentiation, marketing by values – meaning **what the business is *about* rather than what it does or delivers.** The challenge for the doctor is to get clear and succinct about that, so that he knows what his business is about, and can communicate that to his staff, and can develop effective messages for patients and the public. **I think you have rare clarity. How would you enunciate your positioning, as you present it to patients, and as different than what they may have experienced elsewhere?**

DR. ROIZEN: My job is to help patients understand their bodies, so that they know more about their bodies than they do their cell-phone plans. So that they can understand how much control they have over the quality of their lives. My job is to get people emotionally involved.

DSK: If I may, I think there are some significant things to notice here about what you did <u>not</u> say here as well as what you did. You did <u>not</u> talk about diagnosis, or delivering excellent care, or dispensing medicine, these things, I suppose, a given. And with no inherent differentiation. You also did <u>not</u> talk in terms of, in the language of, you in control. Instead, you talked in terms of education and, as you said, earlier, *motivation.* Not just telling them what to do, or even just why that needed to be done, but convincing them to do it and to do things for themselves. **I would say you are trying to empower patients, not just treat patients.** That may be the opposite of most doctors' intentions, and it's certainly the opposite of most doctors' results. And what I'd emphasize, from a marketing standpoint, is that patients getting treatment, no matter how effective, are basically dependent, passive and unmotivated by that experience, so they are unlikely to turn into referring champions. Patients who feel empowered by their experience are highly motivated and won't be able to resist telling others about you. Dr. Roizen, thank you for your time and insights. We know you are extremely busy and your time is precious.

****

There are two key points made in this interview that I want to comment further on…

1

Let's look at the attraction of new patients or customers through all means. I cited Dr. Roizen's genius in <u>creating proprietary concepts to talk about</u>, instead of having to talk about himself or what he does or products or services. This, too, you'll find in my business life if you think about it. For example, there has been the "accomplish more in the next 12 months than in the previous 12 years" concept, branded as The Phenomenon™. This was extracted from my "Renegade Millionaire" programs, they built on the concept of "secret behavioral commonalities shared by first generation, from scratch millionaire and multi-millionaire entrepreneurs." I built my business on "Magnetic Marketing," the concept of attracting customers to you, rather than chasing them, hunting them down; for salespeople, "cold" prospecting eliminated, for business owners, unpredictable and wasteful mass advertising eliminated. My entire business is based on the "No B.S." concept that became a brand: that with me you get no theory, no "ideas," and no sugar-coated pabulum. In Hollywood, these are called "High Concept" in a way The Big Idea that ad-man David Ogilvy preached. (Many Hollywood High Concepts are built with borrowed parts, by the way. If you remember the old *Wild, Wild West* show, it followed the wildly popular *Man From U.N.C.L.E.* and was, in fact, the men from *U.N.C.L.E.* cloned in the old west.) So, back to Dr. Roizen...

2

<u>The second point I want to emphasize is: he has no compunctions or res-ervations about SELLING</u>, and understands and embraces the fact that he is in the selling profession, needs to be good at it, and nothing good happens unless he is selling, as he puts it, patients and the public on getting healthy.

CHAPTER 10
WHAT EVERY ADVISOR CAN LEARN FROM SUZE ORMAN

BY MATT ZAGULA

I'm sure that headline immediately grabbed you because you believe you are ten times the financial advisor Suze Orman ever was! And I truly believe that you really are much more knowledgeable and skilled at helping "real" clients than her. But guess what? I'd pick her marketing positioning over yours all day long.

What if Suze launched the Suze Orman Retirement Fund? How long would it take her to grow that fund to $1-Billion in assets? I'm guessing not too long. Why? She's a celebrity and a perceived authority on personal finance.

Love her or hate her—she has masterfully positioned herself. So the real question is: can an advisor copy Suze Orman's market positioning in their hometown? I believe the answer is yes and here's how:

Suze is perceived as an authority because she has written a whole series of books on every imaginable financial topic. It's crazy how the word author is actually in the word authority. Have you ever heard someone say, "oh, he's the guy who wrote the book on so and so"?

When I think of authority I think of expert witnesses. My father was a very successful trial lawyer. I believe a big part of his success can be traced back to his genius in finding and hiring "the guy who wrote the book" as his expert witness. Imagine a scenario where the other side's expert witness is referring to the *William's Pediatric Guide* to prove their case and my dear old dad's expert is Williams, the author of the book, telling them why they are wrong. So, the guy who wrote the book is the definitive expert.

Suze is also a celebrity. She's on TV all the time. Being a celebrity is powerful. The public places great value in celebrity status. Look at what celebrities earn. It's not a stretch to say celebrity status = wealth. Plus, celebrity wealth creation often happens rapidly—you know, Lady Gaga was doing bar gigs two years ago. And no greater celebrity wealth creation example exists beyond Oprah Winfrey who is a billionaire as a direct result of her celebrity status.

Like Suze, I'm on TV too, in a 30-minute "TV show" also known as an infomercial. The show enhances my authority and it creates a level of celebrity for me in my cable TV viewing market. Last month we brought in $12.52 in revenue for every $1.00 spent on our "show," and this isn't including the value of the support the show lent to our other marketing methods. I'm certainly no Oprah, but a 12 to 1 ROI works for me.

Both celebrity and authority can be created. Both can be manufactured through effort and/or purchase. Am I on TV because a talent agent discovered me? No, I'm there because I paid to be there. Did my publisher publish my last two books because of my amazing writing skills? Wrong again. I paid to play in the author's arena. Now, I am very proud of what I have created and the content is perfectly in line with my planning beliefs but the exposure was bought.

However, not all exposure is bought. I write a monthly article for Insurance News Net magazine because the editors there checked me out and know I know advisor marketing and advertising. I didn't buy that exposure, I earned it. So, exposure can also be earned.

Business is really all about power. To be great in business you have to be perceived as having power. And the public equates trust with power. Someone, somewhere came up with the idea that "the customer is king". Guess what—the customer doesn't want to be the king. The customer wants to find the person who is the best at what they do and hire them to be their king. So, you, my advisor friend, are the king and you need to position accordingly. Which brings me to my final point: you can spend a lot of money manufacturing celebrity and authority and still absolutely blow it if you fail with exclusivity.

How easy do you think it would be to get an appointment with Suze Orman? I'm guessing it would be about as hard as getting an appointment with President Barrack Obama. Assuming it was even possible, do you think Suze would come to your house to meet you? Do you think her assistant would work around your schedule and agree to have Suze meet you in the evening or on a Saturday afternoon because you're busy at work? Of course not. You are just lucky she will meet you at all and that meeting will suit her schedule and conform to her rules.

Living marketing legend, business guru and my co-author here Dan Kennedy says: "Customer service does not mean customer servitude." Suze offers you a clear road map to success. Honestly, most advisors won't follow her lead because it's a lot of work, it costs money and they don't have the internal belief system to accept a position of authority and celebrity. If you, however, are the exception and can easily see yourself as your area's authority and financial celebrity what a tremendous opportunity this Chapter just handed you, on a shiny silver platter, to totally dominate your local market.

CHAPTER 11

ARE YOU UP FOR A MUCH MORE SOPHISTICATED APPROACH TO SELLING?

BY DAN KENNEDY

One of the differences in incomes in sales professionals is sophistication.

Under 6-figures, most sales professionals aren't very professional at all, nor are they granted professional status in the minds of their customers or clients. Most rely more on canned, simple formulas and brute force. Theirs is a numbers game, either with very low closing percentages, high closing rates for very low transactions, or worse, basic order-taking for commodities.

In 6-figures, the salespeople tend to get smarter and have more depth of knowledge about selling, but still tend to rely on mechanical approaches rather than psychological approaches. They rarely achieve true trusted advisor status. A good living can be made this way, but, among other disadvantages, the effort required to get clients and make sales never diminishes – it is something of a Groundhog Day, having to do it all over again "from zero" day after day, client after client. In the financial field, you see this with the free-dinner-bait seminar-givers, who must sort through hordes of poorly qualified clients in order to find few good ones, then go through a difficult sales process with each, truthfully close few – the average, as far as I can tell, is about 3 out of 10 (pitiful), and even then, the clients tend to keep their investable assets divided with other advisors, sellers and self-directed investments.

The relative few who earn 7-figure incomes, ironically, sustain such income with far less effort because they do attain true trusted advisor status with high value clients, who can and do refer at a significant enough level that the need to play needle-in-haystack with plate-lickers goes away altogether. These advisors, like my associate Matt Zagula, enjoy 80%+ closing averages, less resistance, better compliance, access to a higher percentage of each client's investable assets…for three basic reasons: one, better clients to begin with, from superior, sophisticated marketing and from clients as well as other professionals' referrals; two, a far more sophisticated, psychology-based approach to selling; and three, overall, status as an expert, celebrity-ized and trusted advisor. These three things cannot be the result of an "easy button." In fact, the chief stupidity of the majority of businesspeople and salespeople is the insistent search for simple solutions to complex problems and opportunities. The creation of a high trust relationship with a valuable client is a complex matter. The idea that you can consistently create such assets for yourself with "six magic words" or one, canned, standardized piece of media or, well, anything simple is just plain dumb, yet it is the un-holy grail stubbornly sought by most.

To be blunt, I am not interested in you unless you are sincerely, seriously, passionately interested in the creation of high trust relationships with valuable clients – and equally, deeply, passionately interested in the complex understanding of client psychology and the use of very sophisticated marketing and sales processes that produce that asset. This book was not written for the masses of advisors. Not for 5,000, 10,000 or 20,000, although any advisor can benefit from it. Instead, it is candidly part of a deliberate fishing expedition, sponsored by Advisors Excel, to find fewer than 300 advisors who fit not only a particular high-performance, high income profile but also a particular mind-set that translates into desire to be associated with an organization all about both sophisticated financial strategies for clients and highly advanced, sophisticated marketing, sales and relationship management strategies. Matt and I are personally working with the very best, most progressive of the Advisors Excel advisors in implementing marketing and sales processes far superior to everything else in the industry – but this implementation is possible only with advisors interested in complexity and sophistication, not those eager for the simple and easy. It is a relatively rare individual here and in every other field (and I influence over 156 industries– including most high transaction/high client value professionals, including law, medical, cosmetic dentistry, implant dentistry, cosmetic surgery) who has this interest…who really wants to go deeper with their own understanding, and really wants to excel at trust. Most just want to make a sale and view client-getting as a means to that simple end. I have a polar opposite view: I believe you make a sale as part of the process of getting and developing a high value client.

Only you can know where your real interest lies, on the spectrum from simple-minded desire for the simplest tactics to serious interest in the most sophisticated business development strategies. I can tell you that escape from the "Groundhog Day" existence and a business fueled, ultimately, by your own status lies at the latter end of that spectrum. If that is where your interest lies and you are really open to advancing to that elite level in your field, then you will fully investigate the opportunities that may be available to you – if you qualify – with Advisors Excel and with Matt Zagula as lead coach in this process. For the record, Matt is based in a small town in West Virginia, not exactly a "rich market"" his practice generates a very substantial yearly income, part-time; he is not reliant on the common client-getting methods like dinner seminars; and his face to face meetings with new clients are exceptionally productive, with 80% acceptance of his recommendations. None of this is accidental. I'm happy to have been something of a "secret weapon" of his over the past several years, but certainly cannot take the majority of the credit: he has painstakingly invented, tested, refined and perfected unusual and unusually effective methods that I assure you go beyond the scope of 99% of all advisors in every aspect of this business, from client attraction to creating high trust relationships to presentation of ingenious financial concepts and strategies (that drive client investing in appropriate products). My respect for his work and my admiration for the way-beyond-the-norm progressiveness of Excel have led me to an exclusive arrangement with Advisors Excel and with Matt, unprecedented in my 35 years…out of which is coming a series of even more valuable strategies and tools that Matt and I are developing together and using his practice as laboratory to perfect, then handing over to the Advisors Excel's advisors in Matt's trainings and coaching programs. This has me working in developing business systems and marketing/sales tools for those advisors with none of them having to pay my, frankly, extraordinarily steep fees. In essence, it's an elite "co-op" employing me rather than any one advisor footing my bill. (You can be part of it and beneficiary of it, if you qualify.)

Amongst the rules I strive to live by, one is never to work with dumb or intellectually slothful clients. No sum is enough. It's no fun. So if you are dumb or intellectually slothful, please take what you will from this book but go no farther. My warning is that it takes someone of great ambition not just for more income but for the making of that income in a less tiresome, less stressful, more certain, more interesting way to benefit from what we're doing.

There's a character in *The Hobbit*, Bilbo Baggins who makes it clear he does not like "adventures" because they make one late for dinner! This is good metaphor. Top performance people are far more interested in creating an extraordinary business life than they are being at dinner on time, i.e. not exerting themselves mentally in mastery of new, different, even radical ideas.

If you are such a top performance person and meet certain qualifications as an advisor, Matt has a way for you to get firsthand experience with he and I, and with the leadership of Advisors Excel, in a very, very, very different kind of seminar featuring truly advanced concepts – without risking even one thin dime. **It is not free**; personally, I do not believe in "free." I like the ancient Chinese proverb: man choosing free raincoat has no right to complain about getting wet. I think Charlie Chan. Anyway, it's not free, but it is entirely free of risk. In fact, not only is its fee refunded should you feel your time abused, but your airfare and hotel costs are paid for you as well. This time with us is offered to a very limited size group only several times in 2011, so I urge obtaining the information immediately.

As an aside, I am well aware there are countless financial product companies, field organizations, and coaching entities offering you all sorts of "free." There's probably no day in the calendar year lacking a free seminar you can attend – and many of these entities may even bribe you, pay you, fly you in to attend. Know this: such tactics speak to a level of need (if not desperation) on their part, and to their willingness to rope in just about any advisor they can get. This is not the case here.

Finally, a couple of risks I'd like to address very briefly.

One, you may think you are too smart or too experienced or already earning too high of an income to gain from *anybody's* ideas, guidance, experience or methods. This is <u>not</u> my experience with individuals earning extremely high incomes or of great wealth who are my private clients or friends; they are seekers of expertise and better strategy, albeit highly selective in choices of sources and associations. My clients include two partners who built from scratch a $1.6-Billion company; a doctor who has built a national franchise company from scratch to over 300 locations in under 40 months; a cosmetic dentist with average cases of $40,000.00 to $70,000.00; a marketer of investment/commercial real estate in Iowa to investors throughout the U.S., Canada and overseas – most clients from *Forbes, Investors Business Daily*, etc. and referrals, most transactions from $100,000.00 to $1-million+, most never meeting the clients face-to-face; the CEO of a finance-related publishing and training company providing her with a $7-figure income, up by 20%+ each of the past 3 years; Craig Proctor, for 10 consecutive years one of the top 25 RE/MAX agents worldwide. I could go on. My friends include Nido Qubein, President of High Point University (where I am on the advisory board of the School of Communication), a multi-millionaire, who sits on boards of Great Harvest Bread, La-Z-Boy and BB&T Bank; best-selling authors like Gene Landrum (the founder-creator of the Chuck E. Cheese pizza concept); Dan Gainor, head of Business And Media Institute at the Media Research Center, one of the largest, most respected conservative/libertarian "think tanks" and publishers. In coaching, I work almost exclusively with 7-figure income sales and marketing professionals and entrepreneurs.

What these people have in common is keen interest in what they do not know, and a recognition that there is much they do not know. Their egos do not stand in way of their pursuit and acquisition of knowledge. They are also what I call "practitioners of the slight edge" – at their level, self-made billionaire (via the insurance industry) W. Clement Stone's adage: *"Little hinges swing big doors"* is much in play. The same idea worth a 1% income increase can only be worth a paltry $500.00 to the $50,000.00 earner but is worth $10,000.00 to the $1-million earner. Ten such ideas is worth only $5,000.00 to one but $100,000.00 to that $1-million earner. They know it. They act accordingly.

Second risk: you find me off-putting. Perhaps braggadocio or arrogant. Well, I "throw my weight around" only (a) because I have it to throw around, and (b) as demonstration of efficacy of strategies, not just for making money, but for making a helluva lot of money with complete autonomy: *not* having to prospect (not in 20 years), *not* working with anyone but those I choose, *not* trading lifestyle. If you ultimately attend one of the firsthand-experience seminars with Matt and I, for example, you'll come to – of all places – Cleveland. Why there? Because I live there, because it is where I race my horses; we race 3 to 5 nights a week; I hate missing race nights so I'm loathe to travel; thus everything is arranged to suit me. My wife occasionally asks if I actually think the entire world should revolve around me; I ask her if she's asking a *rhetorical* question. But this makes a point. You, too, can have it all your way. The reason you don't is you're stuck in "salesperson mode" or "servant mode" instead of sought-after, category of one, high trust advisor.

You'll find I'm really not arrogant at all. I often tell people the only job I'm qualified to do, in a traditional sense, is asking if you want fries with that. My greatest expertise is in creating exceptional business and personal lifestyle via extreme client control. Our businesses are not at all dissimilar; we are both in the advice business. I'm interested in working with exceptionally successful people, so if you come my way, I realize you have plenty to brag about too, are an accomplished person, a smart person, and there is no reason for me to be arrogant with you – and I won't be. You'll discover, I'm as down to earth as mud. But I do want you to see the demonstration: someone who earns, net, multiple millions a year in income entirely on his terms. In any case, you ought not let any *emotional* reaction you might have at this point get in the way of your own self-interest and advancement. One of my favorite letters from a client includes this sentence: "How glad I am that I didn't let what I felt about you get in the way of everything there was to obtain from you."

So, my final word: if you are intrigued with everything you've read here, investigate fully. Trust your better instincts. Ask yourself if, despite a high income, if there is room for improvement in some aspect(s) of your business – whether how you obtain clients, how easily you obtain them, how systematically and certainly you obtain them, their quality and value, your own status as a highly trusted and relied upon advisor, the very nature of your work, autonomy, security…and ask yourself if there has been sufficient demonstration here of both breadth and depth of knowledge, experience and expertise to warrant your respect and investment (only) of (a little) time to absolutely determine whether or not there may be a more productive and appropriate support system for you. If your answers are positive, Matt would like to hear from you, and I hope to meet you as well.

The subject of this book – trust – is ultimately the only real, solid, proprietary asset you can develop and own in your business. It shouldn't be viewed simplistically or cheaply, as means of making sales. In that context, it and you are very vulnerable. After all, the client can get insurance, annuities and every other financial product from many sources, and is often under pressure from family members, friends, neighbors, co-workers, employer, that loveable Snoopy on TV, heck, the teller at his bank to "talk to" a provider they recommend. The government is doing its level best to undermine the entire industry, commoditize its products, equalize status, tighten and tighten and tighten regulatory parameters. Specific client-getting methods that worked nicely as recently as a year or two ago now disappoint, with climbing costs and falling productivity. People who think very superficially and simplistically (primitively) about this business are marching inexorably toward evolutionary extinction. People who think in terms of the sale, the commission, the next sale, the next commission may make money – by drudgery, mostly – but they fail to create assets of on-going, long-term value. An entirely different world-view of this business is key to an entirely different, superior, more secure and more satisfying career in this business.

FOR SEMINAR INFORMATION, VISIT www.mattzagula.com/AE

SKEPTICISM ABOUT ADVICE-GIVERS

"You will always find some Eskimos willing to instruct the Congolese on how to cope with heat waves."

–Stanislaus Lec

"The definition of an 'advisor' is someone who knows 365 different sexual positions – but can't, himself, get a date."

–Bill Brooks, sales consultant

CHAPTER 12

CREATING TRUST ONLINE—PIPE DREAM?

BY MATT ZAGULA

As financial advisors we focus on what works and what is proven. We utilize our public speaking skills to find the right prospective clients with public workshops. We also use the radio to broadcast our message far and wide within our community. It's no secret that I love infomercial style TV shows where the host lays our the perfect questions for you, the advisor, to flex your financial planning muscle right there on TV.

I find the most powerful position an advisor can assume is that of an author. You know, the guy who wrote the book on the subject. A private consulting client of mine, Bob*, has masterfully positioned the title of his book to align perfectly with his retirement income planning focus: *"How To Generate A 6% Retirement Cash Flow In A 1% Economy."*

*Last name withheld.

Bob is ramping up his authority, as an author, to add to the credibility he gets from being a well known and recognized radio personality and the area's premier educator through weekly seminars, in an effort to build his practice that currently produces $40,000,000.00 a year in annualized financial and insurance product sales. Bob was recently featured at an Advisors Excel's Journey event. At a Journey event, an advisor is chosen who is a top producer to share with his/her peers what their firm looks like, how it operates and how it attained just great success. Bob wowed the 250 advisors in attendance but he still is striving for more, to be bigger, to be better and grow his $40,000,000.00 to numbers never seen by any advisor—ever.

In an effort to accomplish truly legendary production levels, the creation of trust is critical. One of the secrets to building trust is to have the right message—everywhere. That includes online, as well as, offline and online doesn't have to be scary, or a total re-invention. In fact, it doesn't even mean you have to have some fancy, interactive, website. Simplicity and definitive purpose is the key to doing online well.

So, let's first consider do we want a website or a squeeze page? A website can serve many purposes; it can be a brand building/image site or an e-commerce site. For us advisors, typically it serves the purpose of branding and having some presence out in cyberspace. You should know, I don't have a website. Frankly, I eliminated it based on a dare, a wager of sorts with another advisor. Instead, I use only squeeze pages. A squeeze page technically is a website offering relevant information (a video, a whitepaper, an e-book or better, a physical hard copy book) in exchange for information about the requesting website visitor; often referred to as opting in.

Think about it this way: prospects have sought out your information, received your opt-in "gift" and have given you permission to continue to communicate with them based on their interest in what you are offering. This gives your prospects a way to start learning about you and your planning process so they can decide if you are the best equipped advisor to solve their financial problems.

To get a better idea of what a squeeze page looks like, take a look at mine at www.wartimeveteran.com. Since the page is obviously targeted to war-time vets, someone on Google looking for IRA tips isn't going to end up on this site. But a war-time veteran looking for help paying for long term care is exactly who I want to visit, who I want to ask for more information and who I can continue to send information to on this specific subject.

The information is sent to the visitor who opted in by an autoresponder (a system that automatically sends email messages on a pre-set schedule). For this site, that means 17 very personal letters sent explaining the problems war-time veterans face getting these financially attractive benefits and some of the secrets to unlocking the benefits. Notice, I said some of the secrets; ultimately, the message in the solution is as simple as hiring me. These 17 emails are sent every other day over the course of 34 days. At the end, we offer another series of letters explaining "new generation" estate planning with asset protection built in from long term care—I believe that sequence is 26 letters long. If you add up all the correspondence the end receiver can get 57 emails from us and multiple offers to attend our live workshop events so they can meet us face to face, get a copy of our recent book and learn more about our services.

The key to online done right is the material must have significant content value and be written in a conversational tone and be geared towards developing a relationship based on two critical things: 1) I'm a good guy who is here to help you and not jam a financial product down your throat; and 2) I'm an expert and all of this information proves it.

Go ahead and check it out, but don't swipe me because that is copyright protected; plus, it's really important to send a message out that is congruent with who you are not someone else. So, to build trust online here are the steps to do it right:

1. Set up a site—I'd use www.bluehost.com—it offers easy to use templates and it includes everything, including your domain name, for $6.95.

2. Set up a database and autoresponder—the best place to do this is www.aweber.com—up to 5,000 contacts is only $49.00 a month.

3. If you want to really make a premium site use online video like I do at www.themillionareadvisor.com—it's easy to buy the handheld Kodak HD handheld camera for less than $200.00 and set up an account at www.ezs3.com.

If you are tech challenged like me, just go to www.guru.com and hire a web designer. Last time I checked there were 699 freelance consultants available from about $20.00 an hour.

In today's fast paced world you do need a web presence. But a brand building website is a waste of money, in my opinion. Instead, start building a list of prospects who are interested in subjects that you are expert. Then send them material online and off that consistently reinforces your expert knowledge. Being everywhere, omnipresent, is a way to create comfort in the minds of your prospects. In essence, by being so public you are, in the minds of your prospects, not trying to hide anything from them. Be everywhere, be trusted and enjoy the prosperity that will certainly follow.

CHAPTER 13

7-FIGURES VS. 6-FIGURES

BY DAN KENNEDY

Several years back, I prepared and conducted, as a one-time-only training for invited Glazer-Kennedy Insider's Circle™ Members, THE 7-FIGURES ACADEMY. As its premise, this: that there are dramatic, marked, very specific differences in what is required of someone earning 7-figures versus someone earning 6-figures. Of course, even the 6-figure earner with no ambition for 7-figures would benefit greatly by understanding these differences. But understanding them is essential for the 7-figure earner.

There is a corollary about wealth. From Logan Pearsall Smith: "To suppose that we could all be rich and NOT behave as the rich behave is like supposing we could drink all day and stay sober."

Since I have been earning a 7-figure income myself for about a decade, and have guided quite a few individuals in widely varying businesses, practices and sales careers into the 7-figures fraternity, I take license to talk about these differences and distinctions, that separate 6-figure from 7-figure earners. Much of this fits within what I teach as "Behavioral Congruency." It is the most *magical* thing I know and teach!

In essence, when you successfully make all your behavior congruent with and mirror of the behavior of those already achieving your particular ambition, time collapses, and you automatically and almost instantly arrive at that ambition. Conversely, to the extent that your behavior remains incongruent with the behavior of those living your ambition, you will be kept from it – no matter how smart you get, how hard you work, how fast you run, how angelic a soul you may be, how magnificently you serve.

I urge re-reading and *s-l-o-w-l-y* considering that paragraph.

There are loads of reasons most people never get anywhere close to their fantasies, dreams, vague hopes, income, success. Paul J. Meyer chalked it up to inadequately defined goals. An entire book, *Talent Is Vastly Over-Rated*, basically advances the premise that achievement reflects focused, determined effort more than it does anything else. As somebody who stuttered almost uncontrollably as child and into my teens but then became one of the highest paid professional speakers with a career including 9 year tenure on the #1 seminar tour in America, addressing audiences of 10,000 to 35,000; someone with no college education who advises CEO's; and someone who – by my assessment – has zero talent but a handful of highly developed skills, I concur. But there certainly are many people with talent, and with education, and with intelligence, advantages, and who work very hard who still never get beyond just making a decent living despite apparently sincere ambition for more – how do you explain them?

I explain them with that paragraph I asked you to re-read slowly.

There is Behavioral Incongruity in the way. If it gets identified, acknowledged and fixed, bingo! It's like the strongest man in the world pushing with all his might in futility against the strongest door held tight by the strongest lock. He can eat Wheaties, take steroids, bulk up in the weight room and still be stymied. But if he had that little, tiny key…

Look, I'm basically an ad-man, a marketing guy. I get paid outrageous sums to figure out advertising and marketing "problems." I often take people who own ordinary businesses and transform their businesses into extraordinary ones that make those owners wildly rich. But I will be the first to tell you that the most brilliant advertising and marketing conceivable as well as the sharpest-honed sales skills will not get you and keep you in the 7-figures fraternity, if you are burdened by Behavioral Incongruity. To leave this out of any discussion about exceptional income creation is a form of fraud.

I have specifically pinpointed nine things 7-figure earners all do, that 6-figure earners do not do. I have found these nine different behaviors in 7-figure earning poker players, cosmetic dentists, financial advisors, actors and entertainers, writers, builders of small to mid-sized companies, even farmers. It obviously takes considerable time to explain these nine things. But what is extremely important is the fact that none of them are attitudinal; this is not about mental attitude or philosophy. They aren't even aptitudinal; this is not about having or developing certain skills. These unique nine factors are all, entirely behavioral. They are things 7-figure earners *do*.

It is my contention that far too much focus is placed on "getting" – not enough on "being." This links to having to pursue, rather than attracting. I don't mean that just in a metaphysical sense either – I mean it in practical terms. The hunter who finds he must hunt everyday is having to hunt everyday because he is a hunter. Many never have to hunt. Kings, for example. Kings are always brought their food, their bounty. The little cub's cry in *The Lion King* is "I just can't wait to be king!" for very good reason. In businesses like yours or mine, hunting can grow very monotonous and mind-numbing and exhausting. It is better to be a king than a hunter.

CHAPTER 14

IS SEEING BELIEVING OR IS BELIEVING SEEING?

BY MATT ZAGULA

I've observed that people really truly develop passions about things. Like hobbies. Let's say you love basketball. Imagine how amazing it would be to meet, have lunch with and talk basketball with Michael Jordan for two hours. If it's hard to imagine, it will certainly never happen.

When I was a kid, I had imaginary friends. As I got older, I'd have crazy, creative imaginative concepts that I'd see working, vividly in my own mind. I'd see the idea working. I'd hear people talking about the success of the idea and my visions were in very realistic settings and in color.

For me, I never developed a passion or love of sports. I have seats on the 48 yard line to the Pittsburgh Steelers home games on the club level. Plus, Rocky Bleier, 4 times Super Bowl champion and a good friend of mine sits right in front of me. So, there are a whole bunch of crazed Steelers fans that would give me their left arm for these seats—to me, it's something to do on Sunday—fun, yes; a passion, far from it.

The only activity that I truly have passion for is business; specifically, sales, persuasion and marketing (besides fishing with my son which is my real number one—but if I didn't have the success I do he wouldn't have fished in some of the best places in the country before the age of 7).

If you were at all familiar with me before getting this book you'd know that I often refer to the work of my co-author Dan Kennedy. Working with Dan provides me that same thrill the basketball fan I mentioned above would get from meeting Jordan. Kennedy is the best marketer alive; a real sales and marketing living legend.

I've always imagined he and I would meet and discuss marketing methods and advanced selling strategies. This obviously materialized, it actually happened as I imagined it would. And, you should know, getting a sit down, with Dan, for two hours to talk business is no easy task; he truly is as exclusive as he portrays himself in his books and programs—it's all for real. The meeting was great, just as I had scripted it in my mind before we met. I walked away very excited at the future of possibilities that meeting opened up for me; which in turn, helps you. The first benefit for you being this book.

So, against my normal nature which is the belief that people get the results their chosen behavior brings to them, I feel bad for people who say, and believe, that seeing is believing. I believed that Kennedy and I would meet, like each other, work on projects together and collaborate way before we sat down face to face. I did, however, see it in my mind before it actually happened. I highly recommend you immediately start to believe whatever it is you want to see and just allow that belief to become attracted to you magnetically. A good belief would be that people meet you and immediately trust you...just a thought...a good one.

That said, just thinking about whatever the "it" is you want does little to make the success you desire happen. I don't believe you just think and then grow rich. I believe you think, you develop a strategic plan and then you work your tail off to implement that plan and adjust accordingly if the results warrant a change.

A perfect example of strategically targeting a goal, was my personal decision to become the most sought after, expensive marketing, sales and persuasion consultant to financial advisors in the country. It was a decision. In an effort to do this, I had to work with the highest, most sought after, down right outrageously expensive marketing experts in the world—both online and offline. But it's not easy giving guys like Dan Kennedy money, you have to earn the right to pay his outrageously expensive fees. Plus, going right to Dan wasn't going to happen, I had to build up credibility.

First, I bought a software company servicing financial advisors specifically for their list, then I hired Frank Kern who is considered one of today's great online marketers. He was only available if you had a list of prospects over 100,000 and a client list of at least 1,000—a list, I had just bought. Then I paid him $10,000.00 per visit to help me build my online campaign for my Millionaire Advisor Monthly program. Together we laid out the Millionaire Advisor Monthly coaching program which specifically had an anti-field marketing organization message, by design. It made them all call me. Ultimately, I realized Advisors Excel actually cared about their existing advisors, something I had never seen before and that they put their money into their existing agency force to improve their business. It's also why, for the first time in my professional career, I moved all my contracts to one marketing organization.

From there, I wrote a letter to Dan laying out the details of the opportunity, faxed it to him and then exactly what I saw in my head vividly happened. So I believed it all would happen long before I saw it happen in front of me. I use this exact same technique when it comes to scripting out the experience for clients and prospects. Every detail from how our marketing arrives at their door, to the exact video playing while they come into our workshops, to where they sit when they come into our office, how they are greeted, exactly how long they wait, who comes into the meeting room first, precisely what is said to elicit a decision maker's response then right into my 9 step compliance close. All of these details are examined at length in the coaching program that I now conduct with Dan Kennedy exclusively for Advisors Excel's producers. To learn more, go to www.MATTZAGULA.com/AE.

IMAGINE THIS

You are going to develop a clear, comprehensive "picture" of...

- Exactly the kind of clients you most want to work with
- Exactly the way you want your business to operate
- Exactly how you want to live your business life
- Exactly the level and type of community prominence and prestige you want
- Exactly the income you want to earn
- Exactly the personal lifestyle you want for yourself and your family

...and a comprehensive plan will be developed and implemented to deliver those exact results. The plan will utilize tested, proven (if radically different) strategies, techniques, processes, and tools you can have complete confidence in. And you'll be supported in bringing the plan to fruition by a field sales organization that really works for its advisors and by a unique team of coaches unlike any other. If you can "see" it, we can build it.

CHAPTER 15

DIFFERENTIATE TO DOMINATE

BY MATT ZAGULA

Once I immersed myself into Planet Dan, a term created by Dan Kennedy's best and most successful students, I quickly (and thankfully) learned that I wasn't in the financial advisory business at all. I was in the trust business; literally.

I focused my business on servicing the back end of legal services that benefit seniors in a niche legal practice commonly referred to as Elder Law. That sub-sector of the legal profession was in its infancy when I discovered it and began my campaign to capitalize on it. I studied the gurus, worked diligently to get them to know me, began speaking at their events and ultimately had more lawyers referring to me, from all over the country, than I had any interest in servicing. In a word, I was overwhelmed. The fact that I was overwhelmed with too much business is quite humorous because at the time I implemented this business model change, I had retained two well known, sought after and expensive business coaches to help me find the right niche market. Both told me this was a bad idea. I reflected on their advice, realized neither was ever a "real" financial advisor, fired them both and blew my production up to nearly unheard of production levels. Key point, be careful who you listen to and make sure they know the business you are in and have had success themselves that warrants you placing your trust in their advice.

Too much work isn't the worst problem to have but I wanted to slow down so I capitalized on the multi-disciplinary law craze that was just emerging. This legal craze was no different than when the AICPA told all the CPAs they should do all the financial advising and get rid of all us pesky financial people. That movement, CPA / financial advising model, failed as miserably as the multi-disciplinary law firm movement. Like many ideas that conceptually make sense but ultimately fail, the exact polar opposite of the idea is the true market winner. For instance, many advisors have enjoyed massive success setting up shop as low cost, yet sophisticated, tax services and then "internally" referring the tax clients to their own financial advisors. This low cost tax preparation model did the exact opposite of the AICPA plan and has accounted for exponentially more success than the CPA / financial advisor model, which frankly failed.

The position I assumed with law firms nationwide was not accidentally had; it was calculated, planned and executed deliberately. These professional relationships lead to and continue to provide me millions of dollars of annual annuity and life insurance sales.

I purposefully differentiated myself, owned the new identity I created for myself, positioned myself favorably from the view of attorneys I wanted referrals from and now I magnetically attract professional referrals from these blue chip law firms, often three days or more each week. The clients referred to me, trust me because they trust the lawyer who referred them to me. Done right, trust is transferrable as long as you build your business to always fulfill the promises you make – something we've done well and continue to refine and improve.

Everyday, I work to protect my relationship with these key referral sources. I see things from their eyes and work to enhance their business positioning so that our relationship is always based on a mutual win-win. To gain a competitive advantage like I now have it took a lot of effort. It's fun for all of us to dream about working smarter not harder but the reality of building a successful business based on superior positioning is that at first you are going to work a lot harder, skip many *American Idol* episodes and click off a few less hours sleeping while you build your lead generation machine. As you work towards cracking the code on how to attract the kind of clients you want to work with you must build a professional team to deliver the promised results. I have Pam Weaver whose ability to fact find and follow through is second to no one. This allows me to keep the client attraction systems on full throttle. The best advisors know the importance of "the back office." Advisors who sell well, but deliver slowly or without proper client communication don't sell for long. A great example of a firm built for clients is Joel* and Nancy's* firm. Joel is an exceptional advisor, with impeccable presentation skills and the gift of taking the complex and making it simple and easy to understand. In other words, people buy Joel – it's an easy decision. Joel can move with great speed and implement new ideas to grow his market because he knows Nancy is an amazing operational manager. Her amazing credentials include being the former Chief Operating Officer of American Skandia – this is a competitive advantage that needs to be articulated to their prospects and clients: Nancy knows how money really works and moves, at a high level.

* Last names withheld.

Differentiation can be manufactured in many ways. In my case, I saw the opportunity to expand my footprint into many large markets that, geographically, I had no access to. My business model has been successfully replicated, with varying degrees of success, all over the country. Go ahead and Google: The Estate And Elder Planning Center. The first five pages are dominated (over 60%) by current and former students of mine. But there's a big problem with replicating…

The vast majority of "students" don't show up really seeking massive transformational value. They come to "pick your brain" or worse to validate their way of doing things. That said, those that showed up with a fire inside of them for success have succeeded at epic levels. Like, Isaac* from Richmond, Virginia. He has nearly **quadrupled** his $4,000,000.00 production level to being on track to do over $12,000,000.00, all done in less than two years, as a result of his following my model perfectly. That leap in production does NOT include the six figure income stream he has created for his firm from collecting, paid in advance, planning fees. It's funny how successful folks flock together. I met Isaac from another long-standing coaching client of mine Jeff*. Jeff, like Isaac, has successfully localized my business model for his area and consistently dominates the senior asset protection planning in his market.

* Last names withheld.

Even in crowded spaces you can differentiate. For instance, my consulting client, Chris* has done just that in his bank dominated market, Charlotte, North Carolina. Chris is quite well known, by design. He has mastered the art of public relations and utilizing media to elevate his status. Chris has been quoted in *The Wall Street Journal*, 100's of *Associated Press* news articles and recently *Men's Health* magazine. He also has been interviewed on *MSNBC* and *CNN* on financial topics; as well as, by local news stations. Chris's media exposure offers him and his firm a level of celebrity. As far as consultations go, consulting Chris was fairly easy because for him it was about amplifying a solid message. It's was about helping a good humble and hard working guy who does great work for his clients, who didn't want to brag too much, understand that his celebrity needs to be plastered on everything he does. Chris is a take action man, the day after our consultation he had our new game plan in motion. Chris looks totally different than other advisors in Charlotte who have a planning bias towards safe money.

* Last name withheld.

I can say with great certainty that advisors who consistently take home a $1,000,000.00 net annually or more do things differently. Many of my consulting clients are in this prestigious and exclusive group and none of us are using "off the shelf" marketing materials from marketing organizations or materials created by insurance companies. We all use, compliant, simplified marketing explanations that make it obvious that we are different from the herd of financial salesman out there. If you want to break away from the pack and leap to the next level of production I highly recommend you go to www.MATTZAGULA.com/AE and see if you qualify for any of the programs I've designed, with significant input and guidance, from my mentor Dan Kennedy exclusively for Advisors Excel.

CHAPTER 16
THE DIFFERENCE IS DIFFERENCE

BY DAN KENNEDY

The objective is to establish trust with clients – to a greater, deeper, more certain extent than other advisors can and that you ever have before, purposefully, so that each client is inspired to bring their relatives and friends to you.

The objective is to develop a business providing a great income and foundation for personal wealth with prominence and prestige, respectful clients, freedom from worry or difficulty in attracting all the good clients you'd like, and the liberty and security to conduct business in a manner that pleases you.

Achieving such objectives is possible. Matt does so. Top advisors he personally coaches do. But it is rare. Very rare. I am describing a profoundly different business-life experience. It requires doing just about everything differently. Clues to just how differently have appeared all throughout this book. Matt wrote of chucking the entire idea of using elaborate, "tricked out," glamour web sites so popular in your profession and so heavily promoted by the brand-building gurus, web site sellers and parent companies – instead utilizing simple lead-capture-only sites; many different ones, each for a specific target audience; each supported by extensive, patient follow-up by e-mail and mail. This is a "micro" (but very important) example of: Very Different. I wrote about stopping the common approach of educating, educating, educating in the deluded belief that doing so equates to trust. This is a "macro" example of: Very Different. If you carefully re-read this book, you'll find many other micro and macro examples of Very Different.

If you want the different business-life experience, you need to embrace doing just about everything differently. Differently than your peers and friends in the business. Differently than you've always done them. Differently from prospective clients' worst expectations.

The difference is difference.

Matt and I can assist you, if you truly have the courage and drive. If you dare to be different–dare to become great–go to www.MATTZAGULA.com/AE and apply to attend one of our live upcoming events; held in Cleveland, of course.

RESOURCES

FROM: MATT ZAGULA

Not "The End." What To Do Next...

If it is clear to you, from your reading of this book, that we bring sophisticated information and strategy to the table, appropriate for high-income, top performing financial advisors, and you are interested in your options for going further and into far greater depth with us, simply jot a note to the effect on your professional stationary with full contact information and fax it to me at 304-740-5003 or go online to www.MATTZAGULA.com/AE and request additional information there.

I work with successful advisors with profound interest in some or all of the following:

- Improving stability and sustainability of your business – so you can relax!

- Elevating your positioning – to that of the ultimate Trusted Advisor

- Attracting better, more respectful and appreciative, more trusting clients

- Effectively working with retired or soon-to-retire boomers and seniors

- Business and income growth without proportionate increase in work or stress

- Better return-on-investment on all advertising and marketing dollars spent

- Systemizing and automating marketing – replacing "hit 'n miss" efforts

- Using print, radio, TV, internet and other media effectively and profitably

- TOTAL MARKET DOMINATION®—my proprietary, integrated System for making yourself THE pre-eminent advisor for a chosen target market in your area

A few comments from advisors I work with appear on the next 6 pages. (Please do not contact them directly; they are busy with their businesses and personal lives; their comments here speak for themselves and were generously given without compensation from me of any kind. They should not be asked to take their time to discuss what I offer with you.)

COMPLIMENTARY INFORMATION about my work with top advisors is available on request. If you are a $5-Million+ producer, please request the Information Package directly from me via fax to 304-740-5003.

MATT ZAGULA

What Advisors Say About Matt Zagula

BOB G., FLORIDA

"I've spent a lot of years in this business, starting out in Ohio as a practicing Estate Planning Attorney to where I am today in Southwest Florida running arguably one of the most productive financial planning and tax practices in the State."

"Over the years, I've met trainers, top producers and a long list of so-called gurus and have learned from them but no one person has had more impact, in a very short period of time, than Matt Zagula has had on my practice. His compliance closing techniques and professional positioning concepts are amazingly simple to learn and extremely effective, the benefits to my business have been nothing less than transformational."

* Bob presented to 250 top producers in Orlando Florida at Advisor's Excel's Journey Event – Bob was already over $40,000,000 in submitted production at that September Event.

CHRIS A., RENO, NEVADA

"I heard about Matt from a very trusted and respected source and was very interested in learning how to continue to improve my practice. My interest turned to slight panic when I heard the cost for one day of his time was $24,997 – quite a price tag."

"I took a leap of faith and am so thankful that I did because that day truly set my firm in a new direction. The results, the next thirty days, starting from the day I got back to my office from West Virginia (of all places), I had the most profitable, productive 30 days of my career and that success keeps compounding"

* Chris was recently selected as one of the finalists for *Senior Advisor* Magazine's Advisor of The Year.

COACH PETE, NORTH CAROLINA

"Coach Pete radio has been my primary source of getting new business with great results. That said, when I spent the day with Matt going through his Total Market Domination® process I quickly realized that the marketing message that was working so well for me already (radio) could be so much more powerful, if amplified correctly through other media. Matt helped me through that transition and now I am much better positioned in my marketplace."

* Pete's radio show is syndicated in over 25 cities across the country. Pete works with select Advisors Excel agents to get on the radio and use direct response techniques to get quality leads.

ISAAC W., RICHMOND, VIRGINIA

"I've worked with Matt for a couple of years now and I've got to tell you I am so thankful that he became my coach, mentor and friend. In our office, we call him Uncle Matt because just like a good old Uncle who is looking out for you he isn't always easy with his words. That said, it's his understanding of how to use words to motivate that truly is his golden talent. I had a painful conversion over to his way of doing business; but, once his compliance closing techniques set in, it literally changed everything."

"Us advisors love numbers, so here's a few for you to think about – before Matt we we're doing about $4,000,000 in production annually after Matt over $12,000,000 annually plus an additional fee income of over $100,000 a year that I didn't even know was possible before I met him. Oh, did I mention that all happened in 18 months?"

CHRIS H. , NORTH CAROLINA

"Constant improvement is what I look for in my practice. It makes me laugh, looking back now, thinking about my flight to Pittsburgh from Charlotte, knowing I'd land and then drive down into West Virginia was a bit surreal. I just kept reminding myself Bob and Chris came to see Zagula for a reason ... he has to be good ... but West Virginia isn't exactly where you'd expect to find a sales, persuasion and marketing expert."

"Getting picked up in the white Bentley was cool ice breaker, ultimately, I was blown away by a few business practice tweaks Matt recommended and their immediate bottom line impact: a new $1,000,000 client the very next week. So, I did find a sales, persuasion and marketing expert there in West Virginia; plus, if you are lucky enough to get Matt talking about his CCAPS plan jump on it – revolutionary!"

WILLIAM "BILL" S., SANDUSKY, OHIO

"As a business practices trainer and coach to financial advisors, I can appreciate when someone comes along with different ideas that are effective."

"With Matt, it's not a golden nugget or two, he just flips the whole enchilada upside down and takes a completely contrarian view, a view that's hard to dismiss when you see the success he has had and how he has helped others improve their performance as well, including me!"

JOEL J., CONNECTICUT

"I've invested heavily in education and coaching. My day with Matt delivered exponentially more value, starting the very next day, than year long coaching relationships delivered over the entire year."

CHAD S., ILLINOIS

"If you let Matt look inside of your business with you, he will flush out some really unique ideas for your business. I went from being somewhat concerned about my upcoming year's marketing plan to totally pumped up because the market positioning we formulated that day just nailed exactly who I am and what a new client can expect from me and my firm – he certainly helped me launch the direction of my new marketing campaign out of the sea of sameness and into it's own class – 2011 is going to be a very good year."

CODY FOSTER, FOUNDER ADVISORS EXCEL

"The list of consultants out there who supposedly can double an advisor's production and income is a very long list. I can say, with certainty, there is a lot more smoke and mirror than substance to nearly all of those claims. Frankly, I expected the same from Matt!"

"But at Advisors Excel we are always looking for that competitive edge for our advisors, so I had to do the due diligence on Matt. The results were shocking and we immediately started steering our best advisors to Matt to see if he could deliver results. We benchmarked their production before and after working with Matt and the numbers don't lie. This is someone you need to know if you want to be at the top of our leader board!"

FROM: DAN KENNEDY

More From Me, (Nearly) Free

If you found what I brought to this book of value, you are invited to sample my monthly *No B.S. Marketing Newsletter*, attend free webinars, and other resources within a two month trial-membership in Glazer-Kennedy Insiders Circle™. There is no fee, only a small shipping/handling charge, and continuing membership is entirely at your option. Every month, I and the Glazer-Kennedy Team bring forward a new collection of radically different, "what works" advertising, marketing, sales and business improvement strategies and actual, current examples, news, opinion and motivation. Visit: www.FreeGiftFrom.com/Zagula.

Glazer-Kennedy Insider's Circle™ is the largest association of independent business owners, entrepreneurs and sales professionals with a shared, strong interest in exceptionally effective marketing strategies.

Other Books Authored by Dan

No BS Business Success IN THE NEW ECONOMY

No BS SALES Success IN THE NEW ECONOMY

No BS Wealth Attraction IN THE NEW ECONOMY

No BS Time Management for Entrepreneurs

No BS Ruthless Management of People & Profits

No BS Direct Marketing (for NON-Direct Marketing Businesses)

No BS Marketing to the Affluent

The Ultimate Marketing Plan

The Ultimate Sales Letter

Making Them Believe: Lost Secrets of Dr. Brinkley-Style Marketing (w. Chip Kessler)

Uncensored Sales Strategies (w. Sydney Barrow)

The NEW Psycho-Cybernetics (w. Dr. Maxwell Maltz)

All books available at amazon.com, BN.com, all booksellers. Additional information at www.NoBSBooks.com